Creating Value with Human Capital Investment

CREATING VALUE
with
HUMAN CAPITAL INVESTMENT

by

Michael E. Echols

TAPESTRY PRESS
WYOMISSING, PENNSYLVANIA

Tapestry Press
1401 Parkside Dr. North
Wyomissing, PA 19610
610-375-1422   www.tapestrypressinc.com

Printed in the U.S.A.

12 11 10 09 08   1 2 3 4 5

Library of Congress Control Number: 2007938690

ISBN 978-1-930819-55-9

Cover and book design and layout by
D. & F. Scott Publishing, Inc.
N. Richland Hills, Texas

Contents

Introduction

This book is designed to help executives make better intangible asset investment decisions. The primary focus is on those human capital investments that create greater value in the future. To be successful, the reader will have to be convinced that the investments in tangible assets in the twentieth century are not the key to creating value in the future. A shift in the reader's worldview—a new paradigm about value creation is required.

The challenge is to equip the senior level executives making investment decisions with the insight and tools to create greater value in their own organizations. Data and analyses are provided to support the arguments for the paradigm shift. Because individual company data is not generally available, data for the total US economy is used to make the twenty-first-century value creation arguments. From this macro data, implications for individual executive actions are derived.

The book is organized around three main themes.

1. The *forces in the external world* that are defining how value is being created are identified. The world of value creation has changed dramatically over the past twenty-five years. These changes have raised the importance of investments in intangible assets.

2. The *motivation and behavior* of four key groups of humans that influence human capital investments are examined. The four groups of humans are: security analysts, stockholders, executives, and employees. How the human element of human capital investments shape value creation decisions is explored in depth.

3. The *company policies and practices* that must be changed to increase the value created by human capital invest-

1

ments are documented and examined. New recommended policies, practices, and procedures are presented in detail.

Consider the book a searchable file. Read the sections that you are most interested in first, then go to the other sections to get the data and evidence you need to impact your own organization.

One last note of clarification: by human capital investment, we mean the acquisition of know-how that results from the activities of talent selection, training, education, and experience. These are the investment activities that create human capital. The use of cash and other corporate resources for training, education, and experience are the expenditures that define the investment in human capital so critical to creating value today and tomorrow.

This book will not create value for the reader if the contents do not provide executives with new tools to operationalize the commonly stated phrase:

"Our people are our most important asset."

To create true incremental value, executives will have to manage people as assets. They need new measurements and methods to do this.

1

What is No Longer Creating Most of the Value

There is a general feeling that things are different today. Nearly everyone agrees that the industrial production era of the twentieth century has passed, that we are now in "the information age." Everyday language reflects the shift with phrases like: "this is a global knowledge economy." Such generalizations easily roll off the tongue, but little rigorous analysis exists to validate the words. More importantly, few new policies, procedures, and practices are available to guide leaders on how to make better decisions in this new economic world. A new set of best practices to fit this new global reality are required to guide executive investment decisions.

A new paradigm emerges from the breaking of the old one. Change requires abandonment of what has been successful in the past. Without such a shift, decision makers remain comfortable doing what has worked in the past.

Change is difficult. The familiar tends to dominate the new. "Generals tend to fight the last war." This is certainly the case in investment decision making. The generals of American organizations, the senior level executives, are comfortable with the investment decision rules that created value during the twentieth-century industrial production era. For a century, investments in fixed tangible assets recorded on the balance sheet created real value.

The argument being made here is that things have changed, that investments creating value in the twentieth century are not the engines of value creation today.

3

This discussion begins at a point in time a mere twenty-five years ago. The elapsed time is but a blink of an eye in the history of markets and value creation. To show how dramatically investment impact has changed, a base line for measuring the changes is defined over the five-year period 1980 through 1985. The analysis focuses on the relationship between fixed tangible asset investments and four macro economic measurements that define value creation. These economic measurements are shown in table 1.1

TABLE 1.1
GDP
Corporate Profits
Market price of Standard and Poor's 500 companies
Productivity

In the twentieth century, the measurement and decision rules for fixed tangible asset investment decision making were governed by generally accepted accounting principles (GAAP) used to measure and compare key financial performance of individual companies. GAAP is still being used today. While greater attention will be given to the impact of GAAP on investment decisions, a brief side comment is warranted. GAAP rules define what qualifies to be classified as an asset. The balance sheet is the record of assets, and it is the assets of a company that represent the resources available to create *future* value. The other two primary GAAP reports, cash flow statement and income statement measure *past* financial performance.

For now, it is sufficient to state that fixed tangible assets on the balance sheet are substantive and real, have intrinsic productive value, and are relatively easy to identify and measure. These are some of the attributes that make them so attractive to the accounting profession.

While the balance sheet was a great guide to investment decision making in the industrial production era, its usefulness as a measure of future value potential has diminished appreciably in the twenty-first century. The challenge is to prove it.

80 to 90 percent of value being created results from investments that do not appear on the balance sheet.

Under GAAP rules, assets that do not qualify to be listed on the balance sheet are, by definition, intangible assets. Under GAAP rules, intangible assets are a form of "all other." They are intangible because they do meet the criteria for being defined as tangible.

Language is important. The very word "intangible" implies less than substantive, mystical, as though existing outside of the real tangible world where real decisions and real value is being created. More will be said later about the challenge of making these assets, these "intangibles," more substantive.

To see what has changed in this critical twenty-five-year period, we return to the five-year period 1980–1985 with a look at the relationship between changes in investments on the balance sheet and growth in GDP as measured over that five-year period. A comparison with the beginning of the twenty-first century follows.

To analyze the relationship between investments and value creation, the focus is on one critical fixed tangible asset category on the balance sheets of American corporations. That measurement is Private Non Residential Fixed Investment (PNRFI). By focusing on this investment series, we take out such items as private residences, government expenditures, and such balance sheet items as inventory, goodwill, and cash. The specific investment items in this government series are listed in detail in appendix A.

In the period 1980–1985, the growth in PNRFI was closely tied to the growth in GDP for the economy as a whole. The specific relationship is shown in figure 1.1.

What the data shows is that, in the early 1980s, 88 percent of the increase in GDP was associated with the growth in PNRFI. Conversely, during that period, it can be derived by implication that only 12 percent of growth in GDP was related to growth in intangible assets.

During this baseline five-year period of the industrial production era, executives were strongly motivated to make investments that appeared on the balance sheet. What is clear from the data is that those investments were closely related to creating value as measured by the nation's GDP. Those motivatio⁻⁻

FIGURE 1.1

1980–1985
GROWTH IN PNRFI, GDP
Value Creation and Private Nonresidential
Fixed Investment*

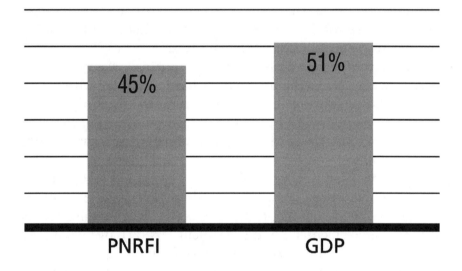

PNRFI · GDP

* See appendix A for details on investment items included in measurement

and behaviors were reinforced by the decision rules for keeping score on financial performance. GAAP rules accommodated and supported decisions that recorded assets on the balance sheet. Intangibles clearly were of minimal importance and therefore could be ignored by both the executives and the accountants with little adverse consequence.

To see how much has changed, it is valuable to move forward to the first five years of the twenty-first century and repeat the same analysis. The results for the relationship between the growth in PNRFI and the growth in GDP is shown in figure 1.2 below.

The data in figure 1.2 show that only about 10 percent of the growth in GDP over the period 2000–2005 was related to PNRFI. This contrasts with 88 percent in the 1980 to 1985 period.

FIGURE 1.2

2000–2005
GROWTH IN PNRFI, GDP
Value Creation and Private Nonresidential Fixed Investment

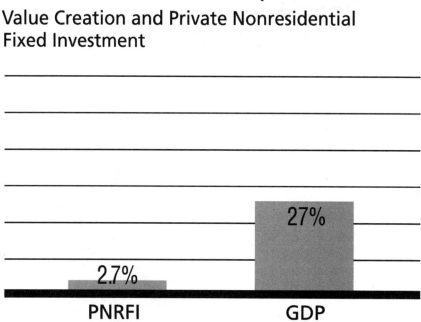

SOURCE: Business of Economic Analysis Web site

Conversely, while intangibles were only about 12 percent in the 1980s, almost 90 percent of the growth in GDP was related to intangible assets in the 2000–2005 period.

The conclusion is that, while PNRFI was critically important to GDP growth only twenty-five years ago, it is far less important to GDP growth today. Conversely, while intangible assets were of little significance in the industrial production era, they are critically important to GDP growth today.

The value analysis does not end with GDP. It is important to examine a value output near and dear to the hearts of senior corporate executives, namely corporate profits. The investment series is the same PNRFI. This time, the comparison is between the growth in PNRFI and the growth in corporate profits in the 2000–2005 period.

FIGURE 1.3

2000–2005
GROWTH IN PNRFI, CORPORATE PROFITS
Value Creation and Private Nonresidential Fixed Investment

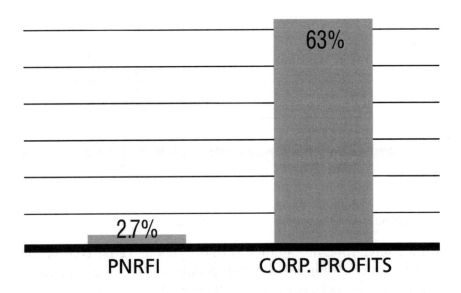

SOURCE: Business of Economic Analysis Web site

The implications of figure 1.3 are especially important in the balance sheet vs. intangible asset investment discussion. The very low growth rate of 2.7% in PNRFI indicates that hundreds of thousands of executives in tens of thousands of companies made independent investment decisions critical to the creation of corporate profits. What they independently decided over the multi-year period 2000–2005 was that such investments in fixed tangible assets were not critical to creating growth in corporate profits. In the aggregate, the fixed investments—and certainly the constant dollar value—did not grow, yet corporate profits grew significantly. The fact that these hundreds of thousands of investment decisions were made independently is important. These were not the result of some industries finding less growth in fixed investment of diminished importance offset by greater investment in other industries with better growth prospects. This is the aggregation of all decisions taken in totality. The net effect of *all* independent PNRFI decisions was that companies did not invest in PNRFI-related assets in proportion to growth in corporate profits.

The other important implication is that investment in *something* contributed to the 63 percent growth in corporate profits. The profits did not appear out of thin air. It has already been concluded that the contribution was not the result of growth in key fixed tangible asset investments on the balance sheet. The explanation is that the growth in corporate profits was driven by value-creating activity not related to private non-residential fixed investment.

While significantly greater research is required to determine exactly what has driven profit growth, it is safe to conclude that at least a part of the growth is related to the growth in intangible assets as measured in the productivity analysis shown in figure 1.5 below. Understanding how to make better investments in intangible assets, including human capital investments, is central to this value-creation discussion.

The growth in corporate profits in the beginning of the twenty-first century impacted the market value of common stocks. While the growth in profits from 2000 through 2005 was spectacular, the period reflected a trend that had begun by the early 1990s. The importance of the balance sheet in the stock markets began to decline beginning in the second half of the 1980s. Figure 1.4 shows the ratio of the Standard and Poor's 500 stock market value to book value for those same companies.

Figure 1.4 shows several important things about value creation. In the period 1980–1985, the ratio of market value to book value varied around one to one, reaching something around one point five to one by 1985. The ratio reflects the continued

9

FIGURE 1.4

MARKET PRICE TO BOOK VALUE STANDARD AND POOR'S 500

P/B Ratio

SOURCE:
Baruch Lev, *Intangibles: Management, Measurement, and Reporting*, Brookings Institution Press, 2001, p. 9.

importance of the balance sheet investments in this late period of the industrial production era. The findings of figure 1.4 for the period are totally consistent with the measurements of PNRFI impact on GDP for the same period shown in figure 1.1. The bottom line in the early 1980s is that the balance sheet was important to GDP growth, growth in corporate profits, and market price of stocks during the industrial production era.

By the early 1990s, around the beginning of the impact of information technology on value, the ratio of market value to book value began to change dramatically. The changes accelerated into the beginning of the twenty-first century, even sustaining the major ratio of about five point five to one even after the bursting of the infamous "tech bubble" in 2000. A more recent calculation of the ratio in February, 2007 for a sample set of companies is documented in appendix B. That data shows a ratio of stock price to book value of five point two to one. This is consistent with the end point shown in figure 1.4. At this ratio of market price to book value, the investments in fixed tangible assets on the balance sheet are explaining only about 18 percent of the market value (one divided by five point five). Again, this is totally consistent with the derived importance calculated for the growth in GDP and corporate profits in the period 2000–2005. This leaves about 80 percent of the market value related to something other than book value recorded on the balance sheet. The importance of intangibles is increased as a result of this data.

The final look at what is creating value in the twenty-first century is a direct look at the impact of intangibles, in this case on the all-important economic-value-creating parameter of productivity. Ultimately, the cornucopia of value creation is fed by productivity. Productivity is defined as the increase in output for a given level of labor input. Investment has always been the engine of growth in this key economic parameter. Productivity is the ultimate horn of plenty.

In the earlier analyses of GDP, corporate profits and market price, it was clearly established that the balance sheet investment engine so important in the early 1980s had lost its value-creating impact by the beginning of the twenty-first century. Investments that were related to as much as 88 percent of value had fallen to as little as 10 to 20 percent by the period 2000–2005. From this, the importance of intangibles was derived. If it is not on the balance sheet, it has to be, by accounting definition, an intangible.

In the case of improvements in productivity, there is direct data and analyses on the impact of the growth in intangible investment. The analysis is done by the highly credible National Bureau of Economic Research. The impact of intangible investments on productivity are shown directly in figure 1.5 below.

Work by Federal Reserve researchers done for the National Bureau of Economic Research (NBER) explores the relationship between investments in intangible assets and growth in productivity. What the conclusions of that research show is that it is not investments in brick and mortar that explain the growth in output per person. The research implies that more than 90 percent of the growth in productivity is related to intangible investments over the period 1995–2003.

FIGURE 1.5

1995–2003
GROWTH IN OUTPUT PER PERSON HOUR
% of Total Productivity Gain

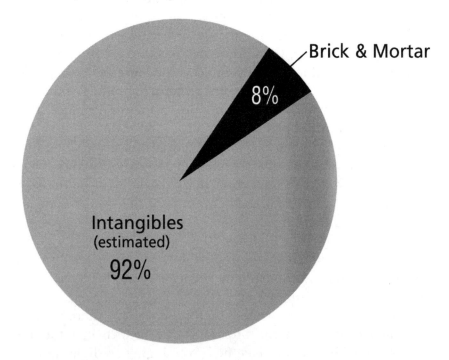

SOURCES:
"Intangible Capital and Economic Growth," Carol Corrado, Charles R. Hulten, and Daniel E. Sichel; NBER Working Paper No. 11948

What makes this analysis so important is that it is a direct analysis of data on intangibles and their relationship to productivity growth. The researchers actually defined and measured the investment in various intangible classifications to assess the economic impact. Details on those intangibles measured in this research are listed in figure 4.3 in chapter 4, titled "Intangibles."

The implications for investment impact on all four value creation economic measurements, GDP, corporate profits, stock market value, and productivity is the same. By the beginning of the twenty-first century, investments in tangible assets, i.e., those appearing on the balance sheet, had gone from about 80 to 90 percent in significance to 10 to 20 percent significance, depending on the value measurement being analyzed. The basic conclusion is the same for all four value measures. Investments so important in the industrial production age are significantly less critical today. The investments that have become important to value creation are those investments classified as intangible assets—those that do not appear on the balance sheet and are *not* covered by GAAP practices and procedures.

It is extremely important to create measurements and analyses to guide better human capital investments, ones that create more value over time. In spite of these implications, it will be shown that current investment practices apply pitifully few resources to this important measurement and analysis activity.

The Mystery of Cash and Global Liquidity in the Twenty-First Century

By extending the value creation analyses of chapter 1, an understanding of the global liquidity mystery begins to emerge. A return to a comparison of the two key periods 1980–1985 and 2000–2005 provides new evidence.

Individual executives allocating resources to private nonresidential fixed investments (PNRFI) did not see such investments as critical to creating value. Those hundreds of thousands of independent investment decisions are affirmed by the GDP and corporate profit analyses shown in figures 1.2 and 1.3. Both value measurements continued to grow in spite of the slowed growth in PNRFI. The second inference is that these same executives did not believe that PNRFI was critical to future earnings growth under the relationship that fixed tangible asset investments today impact corporate earnings in the future, but on a lagged basis. Had these same executives seen such fixed tangible asset investments as critical to the future, they would have made the needed expenditures during the analysis period. As a side note, it is worth observing that these forward-looking decisions were validated by events in 2006.

The fourth quarter of 2006 represented the fourteenth straight quarter when companies in the Standard and Poor's 500 reported double digit earnings per share growth over the same period reported in the prior year. In that same quarter, business investment in tangible assets actually declined.

Comparison of the PNRFI growth and the corporate earnings growth gives some clues about the liquidity mystery. What is clear is that the increased earnings were not reinvested in the PNRFI on the balance sheet. At the same time, inventories of private companies grew only 24 percent over the same period. If the growth in earnings were not expended for PNRFI and almost 40 percentage points of earnings growth were residual after increases in inventory, there is only one balance sheet category left. It is cash.

In the first six years of the twenty-first century, liquidity increased rapidly on individual corporate balance sheets. As recently as the first quarter of 2007, the gusher of cash continued on corporate balance sheets. In the first quarter of 2007, the cash gusher totaled $1.1 trillion, a sufficient level to finance all of the tangible asset investment for corporate capital spending.

Much of the recent corporate borrowing has gone to buy back stock, and, even though corporate borrowing has increased, debt as a share of corporate net worth remains at low levels not seen in two decades. The result is that corporate equity outstanding has dropped by one trillion dollars over the past two years. ("Business Outlook," *Business Week*, June 25, 2007, p. 26.)

Another way to look at the increase in cash is through direct examination of the growth in PNRFI. In figure 2.1 below, we see growth in PNRFI compared to the growth rate in the same series in the 1980–1985 period.

FIGURE 2.1

REAL NONRESIDENTIAL FIXED INVEST (RNRFI)
Nominal dollars in billions

2000 investment	$ 1,232		
2005 investment	1,266	1,734	2005 investment were it at 1980-85 growth rate of 45%
Growth 2005 over 2000	34	554	Growth 2000-2005 if at same 1980-85 growth rate of 45%

What the data in figure 2.1 shows is that about $520 billion of real nonresidential fixed investment (RNRFI) in 2005 alone would have been made if such investments had been made at the 1980–1985 period pace. While it could be argued that some portion of that incremental investment would have been financed by new debt, it is useful to look at the total as though it were all financed out of cash on the balance sheets of American companies. This is the cash created by the growth in reported earnings. Under the latter, companies had a minimum of $520 billion in cash that they would not have had under the fixed tangible investment behavior of 1980–1985.

Thus, not only were earnings growing over the 2000–2005 period, the cash generated was not being used in any significant way to purchase real nonresidential fixed assets that appear on the balance sheet. Cash piled up on corporate balance sheets and increasingly was sent back to stockholders in the form of common stock buybacks. As a result, investors no longer were net providers of capital to companies. Just the opposite actually was taking place. Cash flowed in huge amounts from companies to stockholders. Ironically, this outstanding management performance (as measured by traditional financial performance indicators such as growth in corporate profits) seems to have had very little positive benefit to senior management, as will be seen later.

What conclusions can be derived from all of this analysis? The first thing is that the historical relationship between investment in tangible assets on the balance sheet and value creation—be it measured in growth in GDP, growth in profits, increases in market value, and productivity growth—has been broken. Something other than fixed tangible assets are creating value. What is it?

The answer is shown in the Federal Reserve research shown in figure 1.5. It is intangible assets—the assets and related investments that are not recorded on the balance sheet.

It is clear that cash, the least differentiated asset of all, is in excess supply. Corporations are sending cash back to stockholders at record rates through stock buybacks. Over the three-year period 2004–2007, the level of stock buybacks not only grew, it accelerated. In the four-quarter period marked by the second quarter of 2006 and the first quarter of 2007, the companies of the Standard and Poor's 500 alone spent $442 billion to buy back common stock. This sum would have been sufficient to buy back all of the smallest one hundred companies in the S&P 500 index. ("Wealth Hazard: Guessing Low on Profit Growth" by Justin Lahart, page C1, *WSJ,* June 4, 2007)

It is worth a brief side discussion to explore the use of corporate cash to buy back company stock. While such buyback actions delight security analysts, such distribution of balance sheet assets (cash) creates no long term competitive advantage for the company. These cash distributions may move stock prices the day they are announced, but they create no new products, develop no new know-how, and gain no market share for the companies that send cash to stockholders to buy back their own stock. Given the rate security market data is distributed around the world, it can be argued that the impact of a stock buyback annoucement is fully reflected in stock market prices before the end of the day they are announced. In contrast, investments impact value creation in the future, stock buybacks effect only the stock price and, even then, only in the present.

Stock buybacks are not investments. Investment means the commitment of capital within the company to create future returns over time. The distribution of cash *from* the company is actually a disinvestment.

Some might argue that the stock buyback has the potential to raise the stock price thus reducing the effective cost of capital for the company. Such an argument is true in theory; however, since the company already has excess capital in the form of cash, it is giving capital back to stockholders. This is a case where the company is not a user of cash, but a provider of cash. In this case, a lower cost of capital is irrelevant to the company's financial performance.

Why are companies sending so much cash back to stockholders? Companies are giving back the cash because the executives cannot find productive alternatives to invest in operations. It is not seeking yet more cash to invest in operations. Note: in no way does this argument relate to the optimization of debt to stock structure to maximize the results from financial engineering of the firm's capital structure.

What is also clear is that the measurements, analysis tools, and management decision models to evaluate and improve investments in intangible assets are critical to value creation. Better ways to make human capital investments are important to future creation of value. They are also important to providing management with the financial tools to make better investments in intangible assets not listed on the balance sheet.

The remainder of this book examines the investment characteristics of human capital investments. Based on those insights, the goal is to define new policies, practices, and procedures to create greater value. Motivation and behavior of the four critical groups of humans impacting these decisions: employees, senior level executives, stockholders, and security analysts are important to the value-creation goal.

3 Companies are Underinvesting

The pharmaceutical industry spends as much as 75 percent of the resources required to develop a new drug to measure the impact or efficacy of the drug on the patient. Companies making fixed tangible asset investments for new equipment that go on the balance sheet invest 5 to 15 percent of the allocated capital to measure the improvement in output of the product being produced through the new investment. Of the $109 billion American companies spend annually to train and educate their work force, virtually 0 percent of the expenditures are allocated to measure the business impact of these human capital expenditures. The majority of value created in the twenty-first-century global knowledge economy is being created by expenditures in intangibles such as training and education, and the successful competitors will learn how to invest more productively in these new intangible assets of the organization.

Drug development is driven by external compliance requirements, and tangible asset investments recorded on the balance sheet comply with SEC requirements. Investments in new plant and equipment are analyzed using a century of ROI practices and procedures developed with hundreds of millions of person hours of research and development. But learning and education expenditures are based on faith. While faith may have been sufficient in the twentieth century when tangible assets on the balance sheet created the majority of the value, continued dependence on faith is dangerous and risky in the twenty-first century. Competitors unable to manage human capital asset investing with the same sophistication and continuous improvement that companies were able to use in fixed tangible asset investing during the twentieth century are destined to be at severe competitive disadvantage in the global knowledge economy of the twenty-first century.

Those companies that figure out how to measure and improve the return on their education and training investment have the potential to gain competitive advantage in the twenty-first-century global knowledge economy. Those that don't are likely to wither and die. The evidence that is presented later in this book is compelling and overwhelming. Before investigating what successful competitors will need to do in the future, a brief examination of how organizations have come to spend $109 billion without substantive measurement and analysis is useful.

Historically money has been spent on training *in reaction* to developments elsewhere in the business. Training and education have been deployed to:

➤ support new product introductions;
➤ educate employees on how to use tangible asset investments—especially information technology hardware and software such as ERP;
➤ comply with externally imposed legal requirements and;
➤ manage risk of litigation costs resulting from legal and ethical issues such as discrimination.

In all of these cases, the training is reactive and tactical. The challenge is to move beyond tactical expenditures to make training and education investments that are proactive and strategic. Changes in global markets demand the shift.

Deployment of training and the administration of tuition reimbursement benefits (about twenty billion of the $109 billion) have been the responsibility of the human resources (HR) department. Without being judgmental about HR, the fact is that most human resource professionals are not educated in the financial and analytical methods of capital investment decision making. As a result, the advocacy required to move from faith-based support for training and education to financial analyses has not come from human resources departments and is unlikely to come from that source in the future.

At the same time, pressure to make human capital investment decision analysis a part of the financial department's responsibility has not been embraced by chief financial officers either. The reason the CFO has not taken on the challenges of measuring return on investment in intangible assets is because it was investment in fixed capital investments that created value in the industrial production era. In the twentieth century, there was no need to directly analyze the long term financial return on training and education expenditures. In the industrial production era, humans were only an expense—a necessary evil required to operate the equipment recorded on the balance sheet.

All of that has changed dramatically. In the twenty-first century, people will truly be regarded as assets—capital resources with the potential to create a future stream of incremental income. Competitive pressures will require companies to develop new policies, procedures, and practices governing their human capital investments.

Investment in fixed tangible assets on the balance sheet has largely stagnated in the twenty-first century. It is no longer buildings and equipment that are creating the lion's share of value. It is the intangible assets of the organization, largely related to the know-how of the employees that is creating value.

While a fixed tangible asset can be purchased instantaneous in final usable form, it takes years to educate, train, and gain the experience required to have a high impact employee. The dichotomy between what security analysts want and what creates real value from human capital investments are at odds. The very notions of what value is as well as what constitutes human capital investment must be reconsidered. True value involves much more than free cash flow (see appendix E for detailed model of the relationship between cash and value creation).

But cash is the "canary in the mine" of current day investment decision making and value creation in the twenty-first century. Cash is accumulating on corporate balance sheets at record rates. By the end of 2006, the industrial companies in the Standard and Poor's 500 stock index alone have built up $610 billion in cash on their balance sheets, nearly twice the $329 billion they had in 2000 (*Business Week* December 25, 2006 p. 34). The growth in cash is an indication that value is being created. It is also a symptom of a dramatic change in value creation that has taken place in the past twenty-five years.

Cash is the result of growing earnings recorded on the income statements of American companies. By the fourth quarter of 2006, companies listed in the Standard and Poor's 500 index had recorded their fourteenth straight quarter of double digit year-over-year reported earnings growth. This record of reported earnings shows that *something* was creating value. The fact that the cash generated from the earnings growth ended up as cash on the balance sheet rather than as investments in new tangible assets is an indication of significant change. It indicates that while senior level executives were successful in creating earnings they were not as successful at identifying tangible asset investments valuable to creating future earnings growth. As a result, companies announced record stock buybacks as a preferred means to use the cash.

Stock buybacks create no earning asset. In many ways a stock buyback, though praised by security analysts, is a management confession that good investment alternatives within the company are not available, and, in the absence of those good alternatives, the money is being sent back to shareholders with the implied note:

> *"We cannot find good investments so we are giving the cash back to you to find your own investment alternatives."*

The challenge for the use of cash, whether in the hands of the executives or in the hands of stockholders, is to find good investment alternatives to productively use the cash. In the twenty-first century, the majority of those good investment alternatives are not on the balance sheet. They are intangible assets.

 # Intangibles

This book explores how the framing of human capital investment decisions impacts the behavior of executives making those investment decisions. Current business language frames intangible asset investment decisions not as investments at all.

It is not sufficient to simply assert that the majority of value creation has shifted from investments in tangible assets to investments in intangible assets. To be convinced, senior level executives must have a much more definitive understanding of what intangible assets are and how they create value.

Accountants classify everything that does not qualify to be recorded on the balance sheet as intangibles. Through GAAP rules the accounting profession frames the human capital investment discussion. The general definition of intangible reveals some of the reasons so few resources are expended to measure the outcomes of investments in intangibles.

> Def. **intangible** *adjective* 1. (of especially business assets) not having physical substance or intrinsic productive value; 2. incapable of being perceived by the senses especially the sense of touch; 3. hard to pin down or identify; 4. lacking substance or reality.
>
> *WordNet® 3.0*
> *© 2006 Princeton University Published by Princeton University.*
> *All rights reserved.*

As senior level executives make decisions about investments in intangibles in general and human capital investments in particular, the decisions are being framed by the definition shown above. What started out as the narrow technical definition of intangible assets used by accountants to distinguish between assets that qualify to be recorded on the balance sheet and those that do not qualify, has been generalized as those assets that "lack substance or reality." The other expressions of the definition further exacerbate the problem with phrases like: "not having intrinsic productive value," "hard to pin down or identify."

All of these definitions move the senior level executive to the conclusion that intangible assets are not real and have no intrinsic value. Once that intuitive bridge is crossed, expenditures related to measuring, evaluating, and assessing the impact of such expenditures are seen as wasteful. This is one way we have arrived at the current state of affairs where executives are willing to spend $109 billion for training and education but unwilling to spend any money to do what pharmaceutical companies do routinely, namely, to commit resources to design experiments, capture data, and analyze results to make better investment decisions in the future.

The paradigm that human capital investments are too critically important to not devote resources to measure and evaluate the business impact of those investments is at the heart of this discussion. If the book accomplishes nothing more than making the compelling case to change the motivation and behavior of executives to commit such resources it will be a success.

The data in chapter 1 shows that the strong link between the growth in private nonresidential fixed investment (balance sheet assets) and four key economic value outcomes shifted dramatically in the twenty-five-year period between the early 1980s and the first five years of the twenty-first century. Growth in these balance sheet investments tracked closely with GDP growth in the early 1980s, but the linkage was broken in early years of the twenty-first century. The question this raises is: "If investments in fixed assets on the balance sheets of private companies no longer are the primary form of investment growth creating value, what is creating the very favorable value creation outcomes seen in the 2000–2005 period?" The answer is: *investments that do not get recorded on the balance sheet.* By definition, under GAAP rules, these are the intangible assets of the enterprise.

The first challenge is to reverse the three notions of the definition of intangible shown in table 4.1

TABLE 4.1
Myths about Intangible Assets
Myth 1: Intangible assets lack substance or reality
Myth 2: Intangible assets have no intrinsic productive value
Myth 3: Intangible assets are hard to pin down or identify

The Death of Myths 1 and 3

In a National Bureau of Economic Research (NBER) paper titled "Measuring Capital and Technology: an Expanded Framework" written by two Federal Reserve Board researchers and a scientist at the University of Maryland, the researchers defined classes of intangible assets used in the analysis of productivity shown in figure 1.5. In that research, classes of intangibles are defined and measured. The definition of the various intangible asset categories used by the researchers are listed in table 4.2. These classifications and the associated measurements for each destroys the notion that intangible assets are hard to pin down and identify and lack substance or reality. The measurements for each of the classifications shown in table 4.2 are quantified in figure 4.1. Not only did the researchers find the expenditures real, they found them substantive, indeed in magnitude these investments are every bit as large as investments in fixed tangible assets recorded on balance sheets by the beginning of the twenty-first century.

> "Business fixed investment in intangibles was at least as large as business investment in traditional, tangible capital" (p. 5).

The Death of Myth 2

The body of chapter 1 deals with the value created by investments in intangible assets. For GDP, corporate profits, and stock market price, the inference that intangible assets have value is a deduced conclusion. For productivity growth, the very essence of intrinsic productive value in economic systems, figure 1.5 directly demonstrates that it is the investment in intangibles that has created the majority of productivity growth. The unavoidable conclusion is that intangible assets have great intrinsic productive value.

TABLE 4.2

BUSINESS INTANGIBLES BY BROAD GROUP		
Name of Group	**Type of Knowledge Capital**	**Current Status in the NIPAs***
Computerized Information	Knowledge embedded in computer programs and databases	Major component, Computer software is capitalized
Scientific and creative Property	Knowledge acquired through scientific R&D and nonscientific inventive and creative activities	Most scientific and nonscientific R&D is expensed
Economic competencies	Knowledge embedded in firm-specific human and structural resources, including brand names	No items in this category are recognize as assets of the firm

*Note: NIPA—National Income and Product Accounts (NIPA) report the monetary value and sources of output produced in a country and the distribution of incomes that production generates. Data are available at the national and industry level.

SOURCE: Measuring Capital and Technology: An Expanded Framework, Carol Corrado, Charles R. Hulten, and Daniel E. Sichel, Finance and Economics Discussion Series 2004-65; Divisions of Research & Statistics Monetary Affairs, Federal Reserve Board, Washington, DC, August, 2004, p. 40.

A question likely to emerge at this point is: "if intangible assets are so important, why hasn't more work been done to understand the financial impact of such investments"? What the reader needs to realize is that the rapid increase in the importance of intangibles has occurred largely in the past twenty-five years. The rate of those changes can be seen in the slope of the curve in figure 1.4. Even within those twenty-five years, the greatest acceleration, a doubling, has occurred in the most recent ten-year period. Given this rapidly changing economic reality, it is not surprising that the development of a science to measure the impact of intangible asset investments, including human capital investments, is in the earliest stages of development.

The category of intangible asset classifications listed in table 4.2 most critical to the issue of value creation from human capital investments is the category "economic competencies." The NBER researchers defined these as "firm-specific," probably in an attempt to capture the knowledge in business models, products, and markets specific to a firm, along with the experience gained from working at that firm. While it is helpful to look at the modifier "firm-specific" the phrase is too narrow for the human capital investment discussion here. The skills, knowledge, and experience gained in one firm are largely assets of the individual and as such can be applied to firms other than that of the investing organization.

One inference is that the measurements on intangibles labeled as economic competencies in table 4.2 correspond to human capital assets. Of equal importance is the fact that none of these assets appear as contributing to the GDP accounts as stated in table 4.2. Nor do the expenditures appear on the balance sheet of companies, a fact easily confirmed by the examination of any audited GAAP qualifying balance sheet of any American firm. No balance sheet is published with a asset category titled Human Capital.

Figure 4.1 below shows the relationship between productivity growth and the growth in investment in intangible assets. It contains some important facts. The first is that, by 2000, the total annual investment in intangible assets was growing rapidly and, by 2000, had reached a level of $1,220*. In 2000, the private fixed nonresidential investment was $1,232, making investments in intangibles of equal magnitude comparable to capital investment in productive assets recorded on the balance sheet. The second conclusion from figure 4.1 is that investments in economic competencies are more than half of the total investment in intangibles as measured in the NBER research.

---

*Note: Given the newness of the research, the single number is actually an estimate within an estimated range of $1,005–$1,465, a reflection of the primitive state of measurement in this area of the economy.

FIGURE 4.1
INVESTMENT SIZE & GROWTH
(Average over period in billions)

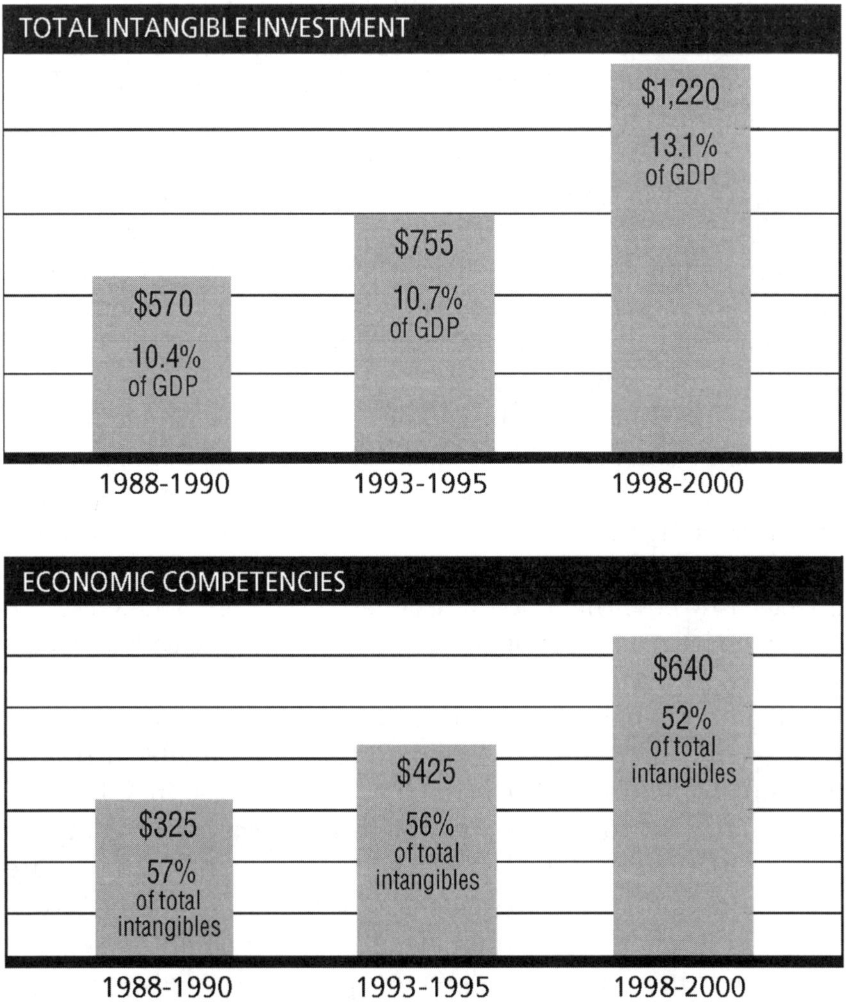

TOTAL INTANGIBLE INVESTMENT

$570 10.4% of GDP	$755 10.7% of GDP	$1,220 13.1% of GDP
1988-1990	1993-1995	1998-2000

ECONOMIC COMPETENCIES

$325 57% of total intangibles	$425 56% of total intangibles	$640 52% of total intangibles
1988-1990	1993-1995	1998-2000

SOURCES: *Measuring Capital and Technology: An Expanded Framework*, Carol Corrado, Charles R. Hulten, and Daniel E. Sichel, Finance and Economics Discussion Series; Divisions of Research & Statistics Monetary Affairs, Federal Reserve Board, Washington, DC, August, 2004

One closing note about this intangibles discussion is warranted at this point. The entire discussion is not an attempt to influence the accounting profession on how to record investments on the balance sheet. Nor is it an attempt to influence federal tax policy. Rules governing the balance sheet are issues only the accountants can resolve among themselves. What this chapter, in combination with chapter 1 shows, is that investments in intangible assets, as classified by accountants, are substantive, real, and measurable. Chapter 1 examined the impact of investments in intangibles on value creation. This chapter shows what such investments are and where they are being made. The challenge in the human capital investment conversation is to avoid trying to redirect the accountants. The accountants are going their own way for their own reasons. The important focus is to make better human capital investment decisions *independent* of how the accountants record those investments or the federal government treats them under tax policy.

5 GAAP and Intangibles

Some argue that investments in human capital cannot be *managed* as investments because the expenditures can't be booked to the balance sheet under current GAAP rules. The implication is that if the accountants don't agree, leaders cannot manage the company's "most important asset (people)" as an asset that creates future value. High levels of turnover at the senior executive level indicate that stockholders believe that senior level executives need to consider strategic issues that deal with investment and value creation beyond existing accounting rules.

The entire GAAP issue must be addressed head on. It will be years before the accounting profession forms a consensus on how to account for intangible assets no matter how compelling the economic evidence is about their importance. In the case of human capital, the existence of free will currently intercedes between the objective criterion so cherished by the accounting profession and recording such assets on the balance sheet. In the meantime, the shift from tangible to intangible assets as the primary value driver continues the accelerating trend of the past twenty-five years.

In reality, senior level executives are already strategically managing assets not recorded on the balance sheet—the intangibles of the organization. A few examples help make the case.

In the oil and gas industry, the balance sheet clearly fails to capture the total value of an oil and gas company. Measurements of hydrocarbon reserves are recognized as even more important than the assets on the balance sheet. Examination of the Exxon Mobil annual report supports the case. On the Exxon Mobil balance sheet are listed the traditional asset categories of cash, receivables, net plant, and equipment. At year end, 2004 net assets on the Exxon Mobil balance sheet totaled approximately $195 billion in value. While this is a considerable sum, it fails to capture the true value of the company. Without reserves of gas and oil in the ground, all of the assets on the balance sheet have little or no value to the stockholders of the company. Refineries are useless if they have no oil to input. The most valuable assets in the oil and gas industry are the reserves under leases and agreements of the enterprise.

In the case of Exxon Mobil, at $65 a barrel, the reserves had a total value of more than $827 billion. Thus the value of the reserves accounts for more than 81 percent of the total asset value of reserves plus the net assets on the balance sheet, even though the accountants refuse to look at the total assets in this fashion. In the oil and gas industry, the importance of the reserves in the value calculation is clearly recognized. The annual report not only documents the level of reserves, but clearly tracks changes in those "intangible" assets even though they are not listed on the balance sheet. The accounting profession has developed additional metrics and measurements to relate the measurements of reserves to future value, the essence of the investment calculation.

The point is that the reserves, probably the most important asset in the oil and gas business, are managed and analyzed along with estimates of future cash flow because these are the assets and associated company resources that determine the true value of the enterprise, even though these assets are never listed on the balance sheet.

The measurements and analyses of reserves in oil and gas are done because these are the elements critical to value creation and in turn are important to stockholders. Without the measurement and related analyses of reserves, it would be impossible for the managers of an oil and gas company to make good investment decisions, let alone communicate to stockholders whether the decisions being made were good ones or bad ones.

The lesson to be learned from the oil and gas discussion is that when measurement and analyses critical to true value factors are in play in an industry or a company, managers figure out how to manage those investment decisions, even though the accounting profession does not report the asset value of those decisions on the balance sheet. In defense of the accountants, to do otherwise would render the objectivity and discipline of the accounting profession irrelevant in the industry.

Other examples of intangibles are the human capital and intellectual assets at Google. With Google, the link to human capital assets is much more direct. Google actually has a strategy to attract, recruit, and develop the best and the brightest. The extremely high ratio of Google market price to accountant measured book value documents the importance of these intangible human capital assets to Google's value creation formula.

The connection of the oil and gas reserves and the human capital at Google are directly connected to the human capital investment discussion. It has already been documented that the balance sheet is not the primary value creation factor in the modern global economy. Were oil and gas executives to manage their enterprises solely on the basis of the balance sheet and the income statement, their fate would no doubt be the same as that of their counterparts in other industries where critical off balance sheet assets have no measurements comparable to reserves in the oil and gas industry or human capital at Google.

Human capital is one of the most important variables in the value creation equation and therefore needs to be measured, analyzed, and managed as an investment. In the absence of good methods to manage the expenditures related to these intangible assets, senior level executives are expending resources without quality feedback on what is working and what isn't. To use an aviation analogy, they are flying blind. Furthermore, without measurements and methods that create transparency, those same executives are unable to demonstrate to the stockholders in the market that good resource allocation decisions are being made. As a result, a startling number of top level managers are being relieved of their responsibility, even as the backward-looking accounting measurements of income and cash flow show unprecedented results.

Once it has been established that human capital is creating value, it is critical to move beyond the general observations to an action plan. Executives need new policies, procedures, and practices. Though the existing measurements and methods are primitive at best, with measurement based analysis, priorities can be defined and defended. The pivotal paradigm shift is to manage expenditures for human capital as investments.

6 Off the Balance Sheet— Human Capital

Even though accountants refuse to place a dollar value on hydrocarbon reserves, investors clearly do. The Exxon Mobil annual report has a section where the levels of reserves are published. Not only are the total numbers listed, further detail breaks out the mix of hydrocarbons (liquids and gas) and changes in the level and mix of those hydrocarbons over the past decade. These are numbers derived from geological data, not accounting rules. The numbers are critical to understanding the assets of the company—assets required to create future value. In the oil and gas industry, hydrocarbon reserves are the key assets to understanding future earnings and cash flow potential and are far more important to future value than the items on the official balance sheet.

The first step in applying the hydrocarbon approach to human capital is to define those human capital measurements that are similar to measurements of hydrocarbon reserves. Just as with the distinction between natural gas and petroleum, the level of education and value of such human capital assets varies across industries and companies. A medical clinic requires a high percentage of medical doctors while a telemarketing firm requires none. At the other end of the spectrum are industries that cannot afford to pay for high levels of education. These industries recruit employees with low levels of education because they cannot compete with the high salaries the market demands for advanced degree holders.

We can learn a lot about valuing human capital from the hydrocarbon reserves example in the oil and gas industry. While accountants are not soon likely to enter human capital on the balance sheet, some of the principles and approaches used in balance sheet accounting can be useful in creating value from human capital investments.

One human capital measurement of value is the current stock of human assets, the inventory of the organization. This could be as crude as the number of employees with various levels of education. Such a calculation would record the number of employees who have an associate degree, a bachelor degree, a master degree and other professional levels. The federal government already records this inventory for the nation. This very data is captured by the US Census Bureau and is listed in publicly accessible tables on the Internet. If the federal government can capture the data across the entire nation, it should be relatively easy for an individual company to measure the same groupings for its own employees.

In another refinement of the national data, the US Census Bureau measures the level of education attained for separate age groups from twenty-five years old to seventy-five years old. Using this approach at the firm level would give critical information about the impact on the human capital assets of future retirement. This analysis would provide a reasonably accurate forecast of the depletion of the firm's human capital stock were that capital managed as inventory is managed. Human capital asset depletion measurements would be similar to the tracking of the depletion of oil and gas reserves that take place in the energy industry. This is especially important data given that there are seventy million plus American workers in the baby boomer age group. Much like the replenishment of hydrocarbon reserves, this existing human capital stock will have to be replaced within the firm or at least a plan for replacement needs to be developed.

Just as with hydrocarbon reserves, changes in the levels of human capital assets along with comparison with competitors in the same industry provide data to make better human capital investment decisions. Given that investments require the passage of time to accomplish and benefit from, inventory analysis (along with the demographic data for the age groupings) would give management a framework for budgeting future human capital investment levels to replace virtually certain human capital depletion patterns sure to impact the organization.

In the end, the GAAP rules do not define whether a company can or should capture and analyze the data about human capital. Nothing stops the management of any company from managing human capital as an asset and the related expenditures as investments. What is needed is better data and analysis to redefine internal policies, procedures and practices related to investment in human capital. It is at the discretion of senior management to actually expend resources to create data and analyze its human capital investments.

Only a small fraction of the cash distributed in stock buybacks would be more than sufficient to create a powerful inventory data base for human capital decision making. Given the turnover in the executive suite, it may well be an experiment some innovative leaders may want to consider. There surely is little to lose given the clear evidence that cash accumulation and stock buybacks have been less than stellar avenues to creating value.

The challenge is to identify the factors that would motivate executives in the C-suite to measure and analyze data on human capital similarly to the way hydrocarbon reserves are recorded and analyzed in the oil and gas industry. Clearly, one key motivator would be clear evidence that human capital investments create growth and/or competitive advantage. Such evidence is likely to satisfy even the stockholders and security analysts in financial markets. But with the very short investment horizon of the latter two groups of humans the task presents a huge challenge. The patience to tolerate anything that takes some time and resources, including data gathering and analysis, is clearly a scarce commodity in American financial markets.

The choice here is to manage into the reality that is, not into the world that ought to be. The pitifully short investment time horizons of stockholders and security analysts are documented in chapter 11. It will also be shown that, for better or worse, the motivations and behaviors of stockholders and security analysts impact both the incomes and the careers of company executives making investment decisions. It simply is not realistic to hope that decision makers with investment authority "do the right thing" by actually managing human capital expenditures as investments. To expect such actions is to require mere mortals in the executive offices to act heroically when it comes to the human capital of the firm. Heroism is hardly a sustainable economic model upon which to build long-term value creation.

7 Framing

Framing involves the language and conceptual framework used to approach a problem. In the case of investment decision making, the GAAP accounting principles frame resource allocation decisions. Both the language and rules of accounting are deeply embedded in executive decision models. Those accounting rules have been developed over decades and were proven to be highly effective methods for resource allocations during the industrial production era of the twentieth century. Then as now, accounting rules frame investment decisions.

But the world has changed. The assets that create value have changed. Now it is time to figure out how to frame resource allocation decisions needed to create future value in the global knowledge economy. No decisions are more important than resource allocation decisions related to human capital investments. Language is the place to begin in the reframing of investment decision making.

Human behavior is heavily influenced by language. In general, the language of measurement and analysis related to learning and education does not exist. Senior level executives are willing to spend more than $109 billion in the aggregate without substantive measurement on what is being gained from those expenditures. Virtually no other business expenditure category receives so much funding with so little accountability. One question that follows from this is: "Why is management so willing to spend so much without accountability?" The answer is: "Because senior management really does believe 'their people are their most important asset.'" Based on that belief, the money is being spent as a matter of faith.

The language disconnect begins with the phrase "human capital." Humans are not managed as capital assets. But the language challenge extends well beyond the root phrase itself. The interaction between thinking about human capital issues and the language used to describe those issues takes decision makers away from today's real human capital challenges. Some of this diversion is a result of the accounting profession's approach to measuring and accounting for expenditures related to humans. But accountants are not the only influencers. All four of the human groups impacting human capital decisions have a role in creating and forming the language. The framing begins in the executive suite—the C level executives in the decision process.

Expenditures related to human capital are never accounted for as capital. Real fixed investment (tangible assets) appear on the balance sheet, but human capital does not. There are good reasons why this is the case. Accountants have a definitive set of conditions that must apply before an asset can be recorded on the balance sheet. The four accounting conditions required to be classified as an asset are shown in table 7.1.

TABLE 7.1
Tangible Asset Requirements
1. It is well defined and separate from other assets;
2. the firm has control over it and can transfer that control;
3. the future economic benefits it will provide can be predicted and,
4. any impairment of its economic value can be determined.

Companies do not have control over, nor can they transfer control of human assets. As a result, expenditures for the development of skills and knowledge are never recorded as assets. All of the accounting and decision rules for human capital operate in the present and thus do not even have the multi-period feature characteristic of investments. This leaves "Our people are our most important asset" as an empty phrase without foundation in practice.

In both *ROI on Human Capital Investment* and *Competitive Advantage from Human Capital Investment*, the author introduces the general concepts of human capital investments. What is clear is that the technical accounting term for assets does not align with the general management usage of the same term. CEOs are using the term in a much broader sense, not as a technical accounting term. Their usage is a reflection of their aspirations and values, not as a strict compliance with external regulatory requirements. "Our people are our most important asset" does not comply with Security and Exchange Commission regulations for financial reporting under GAAP principles.

Several points need to be made on this language issue. Accountants are not saying that executives cannot use terms that do not have a narrow technical meaning required in reporting audited financial statements. There is no objection partly because the scope of the accounting profession's authority on the issue is restricted to the audited financial report, i.e., the document they affix their signature to when communicating financial results to the general public. Those audited results and the associated signatures are documentation that the data presented in the audited financial statement is verified as accurate relative to *the accounting profession's* definition of an asset. The profession is silent as to whether there might or might not be a more useful definition of asset that does not comply with the accounting criteria listed above.

Indeed there is wide precedent in language for words to have more than a single meaning. In the case of financial reporting, the language and definitions of accounting have become the dominant language with regard to the word asset. As a result, GAAP principles move to the fore in discussions about human assets as in "management can't do this or that because GAAP will not allow such an action." The issue is that management cannot do this or that in the reported financial statement, but there is nothing that stops executives from using terms or making decisions independent of whether they meet the definitions and requirements of financial reporting. Eventually, every executive team must reconcile millions of independent decisions with the annual report requirements for communication to investors, but nothing requires such constriction of terms, metrics, and decisions while the related decisions are actually being made within the firm. Millions of decisions are made in companies every day without checking first to assure that the data used in those decisions conform to GAAP reporting requirements.

Time is an important variable in investment decision making. At the organization's operating level, human capital expenditures currently are viewed as though they are immediately and directly being reported to investors. Expenditures to grow or expand the organization's human capital assets are *always* accounted for in the current fiscal year's income statement as an expense and are *never* accounted for as impacting the balance sheet. This reality forces management decisions on human capital expenditures into the language of expense control. The language of expense management distorts the executive decision process and affects behavior. The primary motivation related to expense items is to reduce expenses. Expense language immediately biases the resource allocation decisions of executives in several important ways.

Any management of expenses appropriately focuses on how to reduce the expense under review. The fact that wages and benefits are almost always the largest expense item on the income statement reinforces this tendency to reduce expenditures related to humans.

It is important to recognize that wages and benefits are huge current period expenses and thus require diligent attention and management control. The distinction is that expenditures for training and education are not wages and benefits with one or two exceptions, even though tuition reimbursement is routinely classified as the "tuition assistance benefit." As an employee benefit it is typically managed by the benefits section of the Human Resources department.

Language related to training expenditures is especially contaminated by the framing of expense and current period accounting. A high percentage of training expenditures are "how to" in form, such as sales training or compliance training. These expenditures are made to meet some externally imposed requirement. Examples are sexual harassment avoidance or banking regulatory rule compliance. Those expenditures are targeted to improve immediate employee performance and have a current period focus. Such current period analyses tend to support current period booking of the expenditure as an expense rather than the commitment of resources as an investment with multi-period future payback.

To see the absurdity of the current period focus, consider how executives view the value of current period expenditures for training and education. No senior level executive would ever agree that they expect the payback from the expenditures to cease at the end of the current fiscal reporting period, yet this is exactly how such expenditures are framed.

To his continued credit as a value creating investor, Warren Buffett makes a point of using investment language when speaking of a college education. In the 2005 Berkshire Hathaway Annual Report, Mr. Buffett is very precise in his use of language when discussing education.

> You can gain some insight into the differences between book value and intrinsic value by looking at one form of investment, a college education. Think of the education's cost as its "book value." If this cost is to be accurate, it should include the earnings that were foregone by the student because he chose college rather than a job. First, we must estimate that the graduate will receive over his lifetime and subtract from that figure an estimate of what he would have earned had he lacked his education. That gives us an excess earnings figure, which must then be discounted, at an appropriate interest rate, back to graduation day. The dollar result equals the intrinsic economic value of the education.

This is clearly the language of investment as it involves deferring current consumption to create a multi-year stream of future returns that then must be discounted back to the present. Of note is the fact that this approach recommended by Mr. Buffett is exactly the approach taken in the author's earlier book published in 2005 titled *ROI on Human Capital Investment*. That book presents an analytical model to measure the investment value of a bachelor's degree in the American economy. The work further measures the investment value of the same degree to the company where the employee works.

Mr. Buffett's quote about education is the language of investments, not the language of expenses. It is assets that create future economic value. It is critical to improved human capital investment decisions that related analyses be supported by the appropriate language, namely the language of investments. The language frames the decision process.

Before leaving the issue of language and framing, it is useful to introduce some new economic theory to help explain why the humans of human capital investment continue to make less than ideal decisions, particularly in the face of the very compelling value creation facts about intangibles presented in chapter 1. Something important is impacting human capital investment decision making. One clue is supplied by a body of work called behavioral economics. Since part of this book is about motivation and behavior, this is an especially appropriate place to introduce some research that is not contained in publications about corporate training and education.

The essence of the behavioral economics research, a body of work whose researchers have received several Nobel prizes, deals with what classical economists would call irrational behavior. As a side note, it is interesting to compare the words irrational and intangible. Both words have a certain taint to them as though they are less than worthy of serious consideration, a factor examined in detail in chapter 4 on Intangibles.

For the investigation of behavioral economics, it is sufficient to introduce a primary research finding published in 1979 by Daniel Kahneman of Princeton and Amos Tversky of Stanford in a paper titled "Prospect Theory: An Analysis of Decision under Risk." The paper deals with how people handle uncertain rewards and uncertain risks. The essence of the authors' argument is that:

> The way alternatives are *framed*—not simply their relative value—heavily influence the decisions people make.

In the behavioral economics literature, the term *framed* means the way that alternatives are presented to decision makers. This is important in human capital investment decision making because, under GAAP rules, almost all human capital investment decisions are *framed* as current period expenditures with current period returns. The rational economic implications of this

46

framing were discussed in the earlier work *Competitive Advantage from Human Capital Investment*. In that analysis, it is shown that treating human capital investment as expenses and measuring only current period returns puts human capital investment alternatives at a clear and financially measurable disadvantage to tangible asset investment alternatives. This tends to bias capital investing decisions toward fixed tangible asset alternatives where only a small proportion of twenty-first-century value is being created.

The work in "Competitive Advantage" shows that companies using such resource allocation rules are at a disadvantage to those using multi-period investment analysis to evaluate human capital investment alternatives relative to investments in buildings and equipment, the investments measured in the PNRFI series.

What is now clear is that the language of expense accounting has implications beyond the GAAP financial reporting rules. By framing the human capital investment expenditures as expenses, the accounting profession is not only keeping the expenditure off of the balance sheet, it is framing the investment alternatives in a way that has great significance when considered in the context of the behavioral economics research. The issues may indeed be more behavioral than rational.

The behavioral economics literature contains one more important research result. The general issue is that there is a basic tension in humans and other animals between seizing available rewards in the present, and being patient for rewards in the future, state behavioral economists like David Laibson. In general terms, humans have a tendency to procrastinate on matters that have immediate cost, but future payoff, like dieting, exercise, and cleaning the office. Broadly speaking, "people act irrationally in that they overly discount the future," says Laibson.

In the case of human capital investments, the action in the present is the expensing of expenditures for training and education. The return in the future will come from having the skills and knowledge required to compete in new and emerging markets. All of this further exaggerates the framing implications by making the language of accounting the primary language for managing training and education expenditures. The framing distortion is further amplified by the security analysts who frame most management decisions in terms of current period earnings per share. With the combination of these two framing factors, it is little wonder that the human capital investment decisions emerge the way they do. The behavioral economists would no doubt point out that one should not expect otherwise with such framing going on around resource allocation decisions.

We will return to this issue of apparent irrationality in the behavior of the humans when it comes to human capital investment decisions. As will be seen before the last chapter, the data shows that the performance of human capital investing is not getting better, even though nearly everyone involved acknowledges that the skills and knowledge of the workforce are critical to competitive success in the global knowledge economy of the twenty-first century.

8

Executive Turnover

By early 2007, reporters in the financial press and analysts on Wall Street were marveling at the string of positive earnings reported by American companies. Ending with the last quarter of 2006, Standard and Poor's 500 companies reported the fourteenth consecutive quarter of double digit year over year earnings gains. The number was a record. The recovery from the dot com bust saw these large companies report almost five years of continuous earnings growth. Concurrent with the earnings growth, the financial press reported corporate balance sheets strong with unprecedented levels of cash.

Another notable economic event occurred in the last quarter of 2006. The disconnect between fixed business investment and value creation as presented in chapter 1 continued. The annual growth rate in the GDP in the fourth quarter of 2006 was 2.2 percent. In that same quarter, business investment was down 2.4 percent The comparison is shown in figure 8.1 below.

The year 2006 closed with continued growth and value creation in all economic indicators. The trends seen during the period 2000–2005, as reported in detail in chapter 1, also continued. Both GDP grew and corporate profits grew.

While all of the traditional financial measurements were rocketing to new record levels, a very interesting thing was happening with human capital. In what *Business Week* called "Exec level churn" the data showed that the year 2006 set another record for turnover in the executive suites of American corporations. The

FIGURE 8.1

FOURTH QUARTER 2006 GROWTH IN GDP vs. GROWTH IN CAPITAL INVESTMENTS

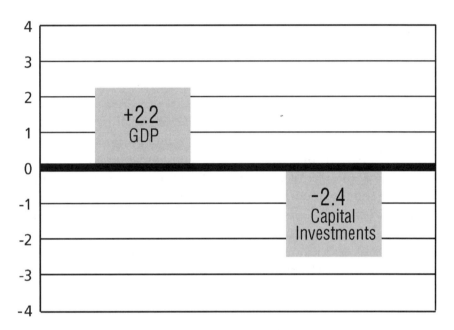

record financial performance did little to assure job security for C level executives.

The turnover at the senior level of American corporations rose dramatically. From directors down to vice presidents, the ranks of the top leadership of American companies saw the turnover increase by 68 percent over 2005 to a total of 28,058 (*Business Week*, January 22, 2007, p. 16). When earnings growth is compared to executive turnover, the relationship is surprising. *They both went up*—exactly the opposite of what one would expect. The conclusion is clear. Extremely favorable financial results did nothing to create executive job security.

Only two explanations are possible. Either stockholders acting through boards of directors were looking for something more than quarterly earnings or stockholders believed that even higher future financial returns were possible than those record results (past) actually being reported.

Turnover in the C suite is not restricted to a few leaders. The issue involves thousands of companies and the career outcomes for tens of thousands of the very most senior executives in the American economy. This is not a quest seeking an explanation for an isolated event. This involves a lot of humans. It involves the humans of human capital with the most training, knowledge and experience of all of the humans in American organizations today. It is valuable to examine the framing of the explanation for the termination of a few high visibility senior executives.

Examples include the unexpected termination of the CEO of GAP that took place in January, 2007 and the resignation of Bob Nardelli, the CEO of The Home Depot. The explanation of these cases, like many other individual executive departures (Eisner at Disney comes to mind) is most often discussed as an isolated occurrence best understood in terms of the personal characteristics of the terminated executive.

On January 3, 2007, Bob Nardelli resigned as CEO of The Home Depot. In the world of electronic communications, a diagnosis of his departure was out within hours of the announcement. Here is the essence of one of the diagnoses as reported by Geoff Colvin, senior editor at large for *Fortune* magazine.

> Nardelli was well trained in finance during his long career at General Electric and he understood what really makes a stock go up. He increased Home Depot's return on capital impressively to almost 20 percent. That's ten full percentage points above the firm's cost of capital, which is a very good spread and something investors love to see.

> But they (stockholders) need more. They also need to believe that the company can maintain or increase that spread for many years into the future—that other companies won't swoop in and compete it away. And investors need to believe that the company can invest increasing sums of capital on which it will earn that spread. The market clearly didn't believe either of those things.

With well publicized actions like these, it is clear that even the CEOs do not have full control over their own destiny. Nardelli joined The Home Depot in 2000 and was terminated less than six years later.

Every other CEO watching this drama unfold before the world is motivated to avoid a similar fate. But the rest of the story contains an even more important message for the discussion about human capital investment. The *Fortune* editor added the following very perceptive analysis to his story:

> And it (Wall Street) believed that the company would be unable to grow its invested capital; indeed, under Nardelli, Home Depot returned billions in its invested capital to investors through stock buybacks, in effect telling shareholders, "here—you invest this money. Maybe you've got better ideas for it than we do."

The last sentence reinforces the message that good investment alternatives are the scarce resource, not cash. Cash is the ultimate commodity and has no value unless invested to create a more favorable financial outcome than cash by itself. A detailed model of value creation and the role of cash is presented in appendix E.

A common thread in the other reports on executive turnover is that the actions to separate the individual executive from the company are often related to the behavior and personal characteristics of the separated executive. In the Nardelli case, a commonly cited rationale for the departure was the so called greed factor related to his $200+ million compensation package. In the GAP clothing store case, it was explained as being related to the CEO's lack of experience in the retailing industry. He was from Disney. While these specific personal interest stories hold the media's attention, they do not provide real insight into the real factors resulting in the total of twenty-eight thousand plus terminations.

Financial performance has been spectacular and widespread. The consecutive quarterly growth in earnings per share is not about any single company. It is a very large sample of the performance of many companies over a considerable period of time. This was not a single one-time event. It was an impressive string of many years of superior financial performance. At the same time, the senior level executive terminations were not a single short- term event. This is another large sample of tens of thousands of very senior level executives over a full year. This is data that cannot be dismissed with a person-specific explanation about how the behavior of one individual executive did or did not align with the view and personalities of their bosses, their board of directors or the company's stockholders. Something much more fundamental is going on here. The tabloid magazine approach to the individual executive story is not sufficient to provide empowering insight. Something much bigger than individual people stories is happening. What is it?

There is an obvious disconnect between financial performance and the contribution being made by senior level leaders. Both the academic literature and the security analysts on Wall Street focus on the role of senior leaders in creating the vision and managing the execution of organizational performance. When Carly Fiorina was forced out of Hewlett Packard, much of the attention was on her supposed lack of vision for the company.

Unfortunately, it is not possible to have it both ways. On the one hand, the tendency to relate senior level terminations with failure to perform financially is convenient. But this explanation is not very revealing when examined in the context of the aggregate data on financial performance and senior level turnover. If quarterly earnings are important to Wall Street analysts and institutional stockholders, what has happened to the link between senior manager job security and reported financial results?

One possible explanation is that Wall Street no longer believes that the senior level executives are critical to financial performance such as reported quarterly earnings per share. This conclusion is highly unlikely since the general stock price reaction to termination of senior leaders like Nardelli and Fiorina has been for the stock price to initially go up in response to enthusiastic comments by security analysts about the prospect of improved company performance under new leadership. On June 18, 2007, when the CEO of Yahoo stepped down, the company's stock price went up 3 percent during market trading and another 4 percent in after hour trading. To quote CNN's report on the action: "Wall Street cheered after Terry Semel stepped down as Yahoo's CEO" (http://money. cnn.com/2007/06/19/technology/pluggedin_lashinsky_yahoo.fortune /index.htm?postversion=2007061911).

The same type of personal explanation was given in June, 2007 when Vernon Hill, the CEO of Commerce Bank, was forced out of the company he had founded and led to admired financial performance. The primary explanation given had to do with family nepotism and sweetheart deals with members of the Hill family, including his wife. In the case of Mr. Hill's departure, Wall Street again celebrated the news by driving up the stock price of Commerce bank shares.

Given this reaction to CEO departures, the conclusion has to be that Wall Street analysts and institutional stockholders believe that the top leadership still matters when it comes to future company performance.

The conclusion has to be that senior level executives are perceived by stockholders to be important to financial performance. Yet there is a major disconnect between earnings growth and senior executive turnover. If indeed the leaders remain important then the turnover must be related to some stockholder disenchantment other than *past* financial performance. American corporations earned record profits in 2006. To conclude that the high level executive turnover in 2006 was based on disappointment with *past* financial performance simply is not supported by the data. The only defensible conclusion is that stockholder concern is about *future* performance as advanced by Colvin in the *Fortune* article cited earlier.

If senior level executives are still perceived as important to performance and *past* record financial performance was actually produced while executive turnover increased, then the only conclusion one can draw is that security analysts and stockholders are dissatisfied with how current leaders are managing or not managing the value creation relative to the *future*.

When the data on consecutive earnings growth and high level executive turnover are examined in conjunction with the data on investment and economic performance over the 2000–2005 period, additional insights begin to emerge. In the end, the market may be right about investments that can produce future value. It has already been shown that intangibles are creating value. Few measurements exist to analyze those intangible assets critical to twenty-first-century value creation. In many ways, both security analysts and senior level executives are trying to measure value when few substantive methods exist to guide and assess the value of those intangible investment decisions.

It is clear that traditional financial accounting measurements such as strengthened balance sheets and significantly increased cash flow did not protect the continued employment of a record number of the senior leaders who produced those record financial results. While accountants may not be concerned about the rules governing the investments in intangible assets, senior level executives being terminated at record rates have to be concerned.

The only reasonable conclusion is that financial performance acceptable in the past was not acceptable in 2006. From directors down through vice presidents, senior level leadership teams need to be doing something very different to retain their jobs. The industrial production era value creation, as measured on balance sheets and cash flow statements, are clearly not what is being valued today.

Both the macro economic data and the financial statements lead to the same fundamental implication. In the American economy, the majority of new value creation is related by something other than traditional investments in fixed tangible assets recorded on the corporate balance sheet. Data from multiple sources indicate that new value is being created by investments other than those recorded on the balance sheet. By accounting definition, these are the intangible assets of the corporation. These are "assets" of the corporation, including the people as in "people are our most important asset."

Unfortunately, the accountants are not helping the cause of the senior leadership. By doggedly sticking to the historical approach for recording and valuing assets, senior leaders are paying a high price for making management decisions based on industrial production era standards. Senior leaders are left without good navigational tools to steer their organizations through the turbulent waters of global markets and aggressive new competitors. From the 2006 executive turnover data, it is clear that today's captains of industry are in need of significantly improved management practices, policies, and procedures to guide investment decisions related to intangible assets. Their careers depend upon it.

9

CEO Vulnerabilities—
Not a Hypothetical Issue

The famous phrase: "The Buck Stops Here" applies to the role C suite executives play in human capital investment decisions. Between the functions of human resources, finance, and the chief executive, the investment decisions are being made that directly impact future value creation. There is a strong case to be made for doing things differently.

By any standard, it has been shown that things are not going well in the C suite. The financial performance that was valued in the past clearly has significantly less value to stockholders today. New challenges have emerged. Corporate finance managers are struggling with massive positive cash flow and are being challenged to find a better use for the liquid assets of the corporation. Recently, the preferred option has been to buy back the common stock of the company.

Even though security analysts love to see positive cash flow, the fact is that excess cash on corporate balance sheet does not create long term value. Cash has no strategic value other than to be invested in assets that can produce output. Cash cannot transform inputs to outputs the way a piece of assembly equipment can. Cash cannot create a new product. Cash cannot attract new customers nor provide outstanding customer service. Cash is great for trading in stocks, but by itself, cash has no strategic value in terms of markets, customers, human capital, competitive advantage, revenue growth, global expansion, product innovation or any of the other activities that create real economic value. Cash is a means to an end, not an end in and of itself. The detailed model of the relationship between cash and real value is presented in appendix E.

Lest one remain unconvinced of the true value of cash, a real world test is in order. Pile cash on a table and jam any input into the pile. Candidates for input are the company's raw materials, information from the company's information systems, customer complaints, employees at any level, or any or and all components of the company value proposition one wishes to select. Without qualification, we know precisely what will come out of the other side of the cash pile. The answer in every case is . . . absolutely nothing. Cash has no creative value other than to purchase tangible and intangible assets that do create future value.

The first group of humans to challenge this assertion will be the security analysts One of the favorite mantras of Wall Street is: "cash is king." For the analyst, cash may be the *only* desirable outcome of value creation activity. For the group of humans who make their living trading securities on a zero time investment horizon, cash is indeed king. For everyone else cash is only a *means* to an end.

To take the input/output discussion one step further, cash spent on training and education can be expected to produce something that does not currently exist. Today, innovation is one of the competitive goals of almost every organization. Innovation results from engaged humans collaborating to create something that does not currently exist; be it a product, a service, or a process.

The creation of the popular Apple iPod is an example of value creation. The biggest pile of cash ever assembled could never, in a million years, produce a single iPod. The iPod came about because a team of humans took some of Apple's cash and applied it to a design effort out of which came the iPod. In the absence of the human capital required to innovate, the cash on the Apple balance sheet was able to create nothing. In this value creation, the cash was an enabler—a means to an end.

The responsibility of the C suite executives is to assemble resources (including cash) and, through collective decision making, create value greater than the value of the cash by itself. Over the first six years of the twenty-first century, executives in the C suite did spectacularly well doing exactly that, producing record growth in earnings per share. Yet, in spite of this record financial performance, CEOs are leaving their positions at a record pace.

Some on Wall Street argue that CEOs have lost sight of who the "real" boss is, that they are guilty of ignoring the "owners" in the modern American economy—the stockholders. This is really a hard argument to swallow since companies are sending cash back to the stockholders at a record pace in the form of common stock buybacks. An alternative to this is to conclude that stockholders do not want cash today. They want more value created tomorrow.

For now, let us remain with the case that the C suite executives are being paid immense salaries to create value to which there is a counter argument that CEOs today have negotiated those immense compensation packages because they expect their tenure to be short and view their peak earning power the same way highly drafted NFL prospects view their earning power. With shortened careers, huge CEO salaries hedge against growing uncertainty.

The real eye opener has to do with the average tenure of the CEO on the American economy today. The average CEO today is on the job less than seven years (*BW* October 30, 2006 p. 80). Some estimate that it has shrunken to as little as five years. Even the seven years is down two years from two decades ago. This is the same trend toward shorter and shorter cycles that we see in the behavior of institutional stockholders with regard to the holding period for stocks.

In a *Business Week* article that examined the expectations around the new CEO of Liz Claiborne, the article stated totally unrealistic expectations for new leaders. "Management experts say that the newly minted boss has about 60 to 90 days to start implementing strategy." These are absurd expectations. It takes a new sales person more than 60 to 90 days just to call on all of their new accounts.

Why is it so critical to the future of Liz Claiborne to start implementing strategy in 90 days? The only logical response has to be that ninety days is the investment horizon of the security analysts. Ninety days is also the length of the quarterly reported earnings cycle.

The pressures to perform in a very short time are real and represent a clear and present danger to the professional lives of CEOs.

Independent research by management professors at Rice University and the University of California at Irvine looks at Fortune 500 data from 1996 to 2000. The research identifies the impact of security analyst's actions on the careers of CEOs. What the research shows is consistent with the record level of senior level executive terminations in 2006 as documented earlier in chapter 8.

As with all such research, the effect of variables other than those of primary interest must be isolated. In this research, it was important to eliminate the effect of poor performance issues. To accomplish this, the researcher's statistical analyses controlled for the effects of dropping revenues and profits.

What the study showed was that security analyst's behavior had a significant impact on the tenure of CEOs. The results are eye opening. Here are is what the data shows:

If half of the security analysts covering a company downgrade the stock, the odds of the CEO being terminated within six months increase by nearly **50 percent**,

and

if just one analyst drops coverage of a company, the chances that the CEO will be gone within one year increase **40 percent**.
(Academy of Management press release, August 2006)

It's no wonder CEO turnover is at record levels. In terms of the motivation and behavior of senior level executives, it's completely rational behavior for the CEO and the other C suite executives to take seriously what security analysts have to say about the company and their performance. Clearly, Wall Street impacts the behavior of CEOs. The data shows that senior managers put themselves at risk if they ignore the priorities and interests of the security analysts.

So what is the bottom line of all these motivation and behavioral interests? The motives and behaviors of leaders in the C suite are directly impacted by the motivations and behaviors of the security analysts—the humans with the shortest investment time horizon. Institutional stockholders have only slightly longer time horizons as soon will be revealed. Institutional stockholders hold the majority of common stock of the largest US corporations, and ultimately it is these stockholders that decide when the board of directors or the senior management must go.

10

Investment

A t the heart of the discussion about human capital is the word *investment*. Fundamental to the concept of investment is the element of time. Investment is about value creation in the future. Investing is about committing resources now to create *future* value.

> *Def.* Investment : An asset or item that is purchased with the hope that it will generate income or appreciate in the future. In an economic sense, an investment is the purchase of goods that are not consumed today but are used in the future to create wealth.—*Investopedia*

Note that even in this definition, it is the purchase of goods (tangible assets) that the definition focuses on. The investment in human capital is not even embraced by the definition.

The importance of time cannot be overstated in the investment discussion. In the final analysis, it was not the past or even current financial performance that defines the characteristics of future value creation. In the case of The Home Depot one can argue that this was the deciding factor in the departure of Mr. Nardelli as CEO. It was the expectations about the *future* returns that the *Fortune* editor Colvin surmised to be at the heart of the decision to terminate the otherwise highly successful executive.

Time is important in human capital investment decisions, as it is in all investment decisions. Unfortunately, the four key groups of humans with influence over human capital investment decisions have very different motivations and behaviors when it comes to the time horizon of their decisions. Figure 10.1 below shows where each of the four groups fall on the time continuum.

FIGURE 10.1

INVESTMENT TIME HORIZONS

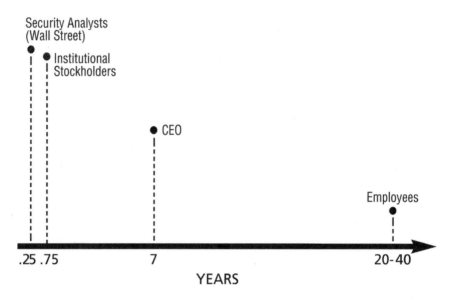

The relative position and order of the humans shown in figure 10.1 reveals much about motivation. At the extreme left are the security analysts. This group is motivated to capture the spread in the trading of securities. The "investment" is the ownership of a certificate recorded in an electronic file somewhere. The holding period for that ownership is now. Long term is a position held over the upcoming weekend. Competitive factors that position the company in end markets, fixed tangible assets other than cash, and intellectual capital are of little value in security trading. Humans are viewed entirely as an expense and terminations are celebrated as positive share price impacting events. The most critical piece of data for this group is this quarter's reported earnings per share. The holding period is determined by the "breaking news" of the moment.

Located at the second data point to the right on the time axis in figure 10.1 are the institutional stockholders, a.k.a. "investors." The alias is added based upon the average holding period of these humans. The terms stockholder and investor are often used interchangeably in the media as though there is no distinction between the two. There is. Berkshire Hathaway stockholders are investors. Individuals who trade in stocks are stockholders. The latter hold stock.

The majority of stock of large publicly traded American corporations is held by institutional "investors." Ironically, these fund managers manage the investment of pension funds for companies and mutual funds for individuals. As a result of their majority shareholder position, institutional investors have a disproportionate impact on the price of publicly traded common stock.

The average stockholding period for institutional "investors" has fallen to approximately nine months or .75 years. Given this extremely short holding period, the distinction between stockholder and investor is an important one. This holding period average puts institutional investors closer to stock trader behavior than to true investor behavior.

We have already been introduced to the next group of humans on the time continuum. These are the CEOs and their staffs. These humans are being terminated at record rates. Their investment time horizon is falling. The tenure is shortening. Record numbers of senior leaders are being terminated.

The average tenure of the American CEO is seven years and getting shorter (*Business Week*, "Executive suite turnover," October 30, 2006, p. 80). This shortening of the tenure of the corporate leaders should not be surprising given the growing influence of security analysts, world markets and ever more impatient institutional stockholders. Recognized as one of the best CEOs of all time, Jack Welsh, was able to lead General Electric for a long time. He was CEO for more than twenty years. Although a darling of Wall Street during his tenure as CEO, in recent discussions, Mr. Welsh has been downgraded in management stature as "old school," characterized as having diminished relevance to today's competitive environment.

Last to the right on the investment time continuum are individuals—the employees of the company. For these individuals education, training, and accumulated experience represent lifetime investments. The learning is a true asset for these humans, and they represent those assets on their personal balance sheet in the form of a resume or vita. Companies review those assets when making hiring decisions. Hiring companies always review those personal assets and, based on the job specifics, the hiring managers make compensation decisions including the actual level of the salary offer. It is a projection of the future value these assets can create that determines those salary offers. Though they do not conform to GAAP principles, the balance sheet of individuals is an important document in the human capital investment discussion.

Human capital investments represent a lifetime asset for the individual. The individual "owns" the created assets. The fact that the individual controls the asset, and not the company, is what stops accountants from treating humans as assets on the corporate balance sheet. Of the four groups, these employees are the humans who have the greatest value creation stake in human capital investment.

One outstanding investor joins the employees at the extreme right side of the time continuum. Indeed he is universally acknowledged as the most successful investor of all time—Mr. Warren Buffett. Mr. Buffett invests in companies with the stated intent of owning the company for his lifetime. Further he states that he invests in management teams. He wants to retain the leaders who created the company he is buying. And of direct relevance to our discussion here, he has repeatedly stated that he invests based on the intangible assets of the company, not the balance sheet.

The four influential groups (security analysts, institutional stockholders, executives and employees) in human capital investments have very different motives, behaviors, and time horizons for their investment decisions. For the most part, expenditures made to increase the asset value of the firm's human capital are not viewed as investments at all, especially by security analysts. They are viewed as investments by individuals.

Companies view these expenditures as an expense with a current period time horizon for most of the decision makers. It is the individual who is most highly motivated to view training, education, and experience as an investment—an asset that will have value with certainty in the future. All of the other groups have a higher degree of financial risk than the individual. The other humans in the four groups, with the exception of Mr. Buffett, view expenditures on humans as current period expenses, not investments at all. As a result, it is little wonder that human capital investments are not seriously managed as true investments.

One of the challenges to creating new policies, procedures, and practices to increase value creation in the future is to understand the motives of these four groups and, to the degree possible, align the behaviors of these four groups regarding return and risk. Measurement and analysis are pivotal in this.

As a result of these powerful forces framing twenty-first-century investment decisions, it is little wonder that the $109 billion spent for training and education are expended with little data and virtually no analysis. The potential to create incremental value is large.

11 The Security Analyst

The extreme left side of the investment time continuum is where the security analyst operates. Stock trading takes place in the moment. This group of humans is strongly influenced by "breaking news." At the outside, the time horizon of the security analyst is the infamous single quarter of "the earning season" when the prior quarter's sales and net income are reported. These earnings reports are telecast on such cable broadcasts as CNBC and dispensed with the intensity similar to truly significant news events.

Though time is a critical dimension of human capital investment decisions and a pivotal distinguishing parameter for our discussions here, it is not the only critical dimension of investment decisions. In the case of the security analysts, it is also interesting to dissect how they frame the stockholder discussion.

The focus on the quarterly reported earnings compresses the time dimension to the present. What is also compressed is the data being considered in the stock trading decision. Both of these compressions work well in the world of ubiquitous information. Soundbites are perfect for the globally-linked electronic media.

Security analysts operate in the modern world of the soundbite. In this world of ubiquitous electronic talking heads, the attention span of the information receiver is short. The agenda of the broadcaster is to continuously stimulate the viewer with new and revealing information. The tease of "breaking news" is used by CNN, on the Internet and by CNBC in financial news reporting. The word "breaking" frames the information as being not previously known and, by implication valuable in its exclusivity. It also pulls the time horizon to the immediate, to the extreme left of the investment time continuum.

In this modern world of media hype, investment decisions that require a longer time horizon or involve complex variables that do not fit in the tiny time slot dictated by the come on word "breaking" are often discarded. A true understanding of a company's capabilities and opportunities takes more than a few moments of attention on a single breaking item.

The complex data that Mr. Buffett ponders prior to making his investment decisions and even more importantly the personal interview he has with his future management partner(s) impacts his decision to invest. It is extremely unlikely that he expects his new business partners to alter the strategy within the first ninety days of acquisition. In fact, the exact opposite is more likely. A new strategy within ninety days of investment is not really even an option. His decision to invest is based largely on the fact that the company and its management already have a strategy attractive to their new owner.

The quarterly earnings report looks backward, not forward. The earnings report is communicated as a representation of all of the complex management decisions made in the past, not just during the reporting quarter. The impact of R&D, investment, and product decisions made years before get condensed into a single number. The reported earnings per share also gives huge weight to two operating numbers for the enterprise—the revenue and the costs in the most recent reporting period. This disproportionate emphasis on the most recent past period results increases the influence of cost control to the detriment of future period investment. The disproportion is especially critical in the area of intangibles where all expenditures are booked as an expense.

In the real world of markets and global competition, a single quarter's reported earnings numbers has limited long term real economic significance. In a world where stock prices impact the amount of capital a company can raise to fund operations, movement of share prices are important to future value creation. Today, in the aggregate, companies are not net users of investment funds. Today companies are not, in the aggregate, raising funds in equity markets. Today, companies are actually net providers of funds to stockholders through cash delivered to those current stockholders in the form of common stock buybacks. Companies are reducing the outstanding equity in the financial markets at a record pace.

What is really ironic about this is the standard to which security analysts compare the coveted earnings per share data and their revenue forecasts. The handful of parameters security analysts report are not stated in comparison to financial and competitive information of actual importance to the success of the company. In general, reported earnings performance comparisons are not made to end market parameters, competitive actions, or emerging technology except in the most superficial and passing fashion and then as a side note. Security analysts compare the most recent quarterly earnings performance to "Wall Street expectations."

When security analysts report company quarterly earnings per share, they report the results relative to the "consensus" of other security analysts. The soundbite reported is given credence by framing the report as a comparison with the "consensus of the street." This frames the report as though it is a comparison with the guesses of a large group of informed individuals. In almost all cases, those expectations include their own forecast of the company performance. Because many companies are covered by only a few analysts (in some cases only one analyst), the consensus street expectation is in fact merely the opinion of the very security analyst providing the soundbite.

This produces a near Alice in Wonderland situation where the complex world of investment within the company is compressed into a few simple numbers that measure the revenue and cost performance and then only in the past. The standard of performance is the guess of the very analysts doing the reporting.

Were the implications not so serious, we might merely pass beyond this group of humans in our detailed examination of human capital investment decision-making processes. Ah, were it only so simple to move on to more substantive investment issues. Unfortunately, it is not. The modern world is filled with sources of instant information. Television is loaded with talking heads. Those talking heads are challenged to fill the twenty-four-hour schedule with "news" to say nothing of the blogs from self-aggrandized amateurs loading the Internet with their personal opinions. All this gives disproportionate weight to soundbites in general, giving the extreme left of the investment time continuum disproportionate influence in framing investment decisions.

Some complain about the excessive influence of the financial soundbite and its messenger, the security analyst. Angst over the intense focus on quarterly earnings per share and the distorted view of near term income as the driver in American companies is well documented. Even with this extensive documentation, behaviors are not changing. With the exception of the emergence of private equity funds, the holding period of stockholders is continuing to drop, evidence that the message from the security analyst and their focus on the past to the determent of the future and cash to the exclusion of investment is very likely to continue. The motivations related to stock trading and the availability of instant soundbites are not going to go away.

The fixation on quarterly earnings per share reports would be inconsequential were it merely a game of security analysts and their street consensus brethren with consequences limited to the trading of shares between stockholders. Unfortunately, there is important evidence that the focus and time horizon of security analysts reaches far beyond Wall Street. The first set of evidence is the shortening holding period of stockholders as shown in figure 12.1. This is evidence that the motivation and behavior of stock trading impacts the investment behavior of stockholders.

The second set of evidence is that the motivation and behavior of security analysts significantly impacts the behavior of the C suite executives who actually make the human capital investment decisions. Were the importance of those behaviors less critical to the other humans in this financial and economic drama, we might be tempted to revert to the luxury of ignoring these cascading effects. The motivations and behaviors of the analysts profoundly affect the human capital investment decision processes in a very important way.

The Stockholders, a.k.a. Investors

The second group of humans in the human capital investment equation are the stockholders. These are predominately managers of institutional funds that buy and sell the stock of American corporations. There is one additional aspect of these humans that is important to the human capital investment discussion. Legally, these are the owners of American industry. They have real power, not merely the power of the soundbite. They are more than talking heads.

The most critical feature of stockholding is that stockholders do exactly what the word implies. They hold stock. In the industrial production era, they actually held the paper stock certificates that documented the ownership claim. Today they don't even hold certificates. They have a computer record of their ownership position far removed from the "blood and guts" of the company making actual investment decisions.

The institutional stockholders have an average investment horizon of about nine months. If investing is about the deferral of current consumption for the gain of future benefit, where do the stockholders of the American economy stack up alongside of the other important humans in the human capital investment decision process?

Ultimately, the stockholders have the legal authority to hire and fire the executive leadership of the organization. And though stockholders process large sums of cash in stock transactions, it is the leadership that ultimately makes the real strategic investment decisions. If stockholders do not like the decisions executives have made, they have the ultimate authority to terminate the board of directors as well as the management. That is exactly what stockholders are doing at a record pace.

The prognosis is pretty grim. It is worth examining the time dimension of stockholder investment decision making. Chapter 9 documented the impact of the short horizon on the tenure of C Suite executives. The combination of security analyst and stockholder behavior is having a significant impact on the tenure of the CEOs leading American corporations. For now we need to return to the behavior of stockholders—a.k.a. investors.

Figure 12.1 below shows the trend in the holding period of institutional stockholders over the past forty-five years.

FIGURE 12.1

AVERAGE STOCK HOLDING PERIOD – INSTITUTIONAL STOCKHOLDERS

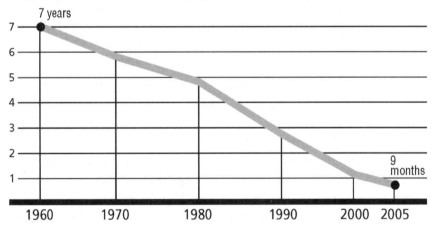

SOURCES: 1945-1987 Investment Company Institute;
1988-2004 Morningstar;
2007 Merrill Lynch 300 international institutional investors

The data in figure 12.1 shows that the average stock-holding period dropped precipitously. Just like the tenure of CEOs, it is continuing to drop. The last data point for the year 2004 shows that the average holding period was less than one year. A Merrill Lynch survey with data from three hundred institutional stockholders world wide reported in January, 2007 showed the average holding period to be nine months. This is the data point shown in figure 10.1.

One might ask: "So what, what should we care that stockholders sell their stock so rapidly?" The implications can be seen by looking at the timeline for human capital investment in a bachelor degree, the investment referenced in the quote by Mr. Buffett. On average, it takes more than five years for a young man or woman to earn a bachelor degree at an American college or university. This means that in the extreme, if individuals behaved like stockholders are behaving no one would get an education in America. Why individuals are willing to invest in themselves over a longer investment horizon while stockholders are not is a key issue for understanding motivation and behavior driving human capital investment.

The surprising thing about the behavior of institutional stockholders is that it contrasts dramatically with the behavior of the universally acclaimed best investor of all times—Mr. Warren Buffett. The data supports the conclusion. The annual return on Berkshire Hathaway (BH) stock compared to the Standard & Poor's 500 index is shown in figure 12.2 below. The data reveals that not only did BH stock earn a higher return than the Standard and Poor's 500, it earned a significantly higher return.

While the numbers verify the success of Mr. Buffett's investment philosophy, it is not the most surprising thing about this comparison. Were it the case that Mr. Buffett accomplished his investing feat under a cloud of secrecy, denying access to his formula for success, it would be one thing. The conclusion would be that he knows something we investing mortals do not know— something akin to knowing the mysterious Coca Cola formula. Were this the case, it might explain the behavior of the vast majority of institutional stockholders.

The reason institutional stockholders do not get the financial returns Mr. Buffett gets has nothing to do with a secret formula. Were there a secret formula, other stockholders would be *unable* to do what Mr. Buffett does. This would be a simple and clear explanation of stockholder behavior shown in figure 10.1 above.

There is no secret formula. In fact exactly the opposite is the case. Mr. Buffett is completely transparent about his investment

73

FIGURE 12.2

BERKSHIRE HATHAWAY FINANCIAL RETURN

Average % Gains (Losses) in Stock Price vs. Standard and Poor's 500 over 5 years

	Standard and Poor's 500	Berkshire Hathaway
1965-1969	6.4	18.06
1970-1974	(.08)	12.06
1975-1979	15.6	34.56
1980-1984	15.4	27.32
1985-1989	20.7	31.66
1990-1994	9.3	19.1
1995-1999	28.7	31.56
2000-2004	(.07)	8.36
Total Gain 1964-2005	5,583%	305,134%

SOURCE: Berkshire Hathaway 2005 Annual Report

74

"secrets." The raw fact is that, year after year, Mr. Buffett documents his formula for his success in his stockholder letter. He tells exactly how he does it and why he does it that way. The Berkshire Hathaway annual report is the pipeline from Mr. Buffett's ideas to the entire stockholder world. In addition to the letter, Mr. Buffett and his partner Charlie Munger sit on a stage in Omaha, Nebraska and for a full day answer Berkshire Hathaway stockholder questions about specific investing decisions. There couldn't be a more open dialogue.

Nothing about Mr. Buffett's investment approach is secret. Mr. Buffett invests in brands and human capital, the intangible assets of the companies he buys. He is interested in the intangibles of the companies he buys, not the balance sheet. Indeed, in an extremely clear discussion about the relative value of intangibles and the balance sheet, Mr. Buffett outlines the distinctions in the Berkshire Hathaway 2005 annual report and at the totally open annual stockholder's meeting.

On the critical investment dimension of time the Berkshire Hathaway investment philosophy is substantially different than that of the security analysts and the institutional stockholders. Berkshire Hathaway deploys a stated strategy to make it less attractive to trade Berkshire Hathaway shares. The stock has never been split, resulting in significantly less turnover in shares. He wants to attract investors, not stockholders, to be partners with him in his companies. Figure 12.3 reproduces the history of the market holding period with one additional data point superimposed. The new piece of data is the average Berkshire Hathaway holding period for 2005 compared to the rest of the market.

What figure 12.3 shows is that the average BH stockholder holds their shares much longer than the average institutional stockholder. By 2007, BH stock sold for more than one hundred thousand dollars a share and had never been split, largely to reduce the buying and selling of the shares. Warren Buffett wants investors. It takes a real commitment to buy and own shares of Berkshire Hathaway. The high price makes day trading in the stock unattractive. BU stockholders hold their BH stock much longer than the average stockholder. They behave much more like investors than stockholders. Investor behavior rather than a stockholder behavior

FIGURE 12.3

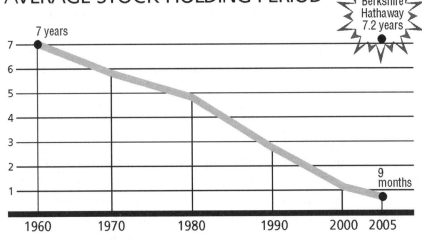

SOURCES: 1945-1987 Investment Company Institute;
1988-2004 Morningstar;
2007 Merrill Lynch 300 international institutional investors

is openly encouraged in BH annual reports and BH stockholder meetings. Mr. Buffett wants a community of investors, partners in the business, participants with him to give the managers of the BH companies time to create value.

There is a related dimension to the long investment horizon used by Berkshire Hathaway. When Mr. Buffett buys a company, he makes the deal with the leadership of the company. Contrary to the enthusiasm of security analysts over the departure of senior executives, he wants the management of the acquired company to stay and run it. That is exactly what happens in almost all cases. The management of BH companies acts very much like the investors of BH. They have a much longer time horizon for investment decision making, including the human capital as represented by the management itself. None of this is a secret. The Berkshire Hathaway motives and behaviors relative to the managers of the companies in the portfolio is exactly the opposite of the security analysts.

13
New Stockholders in the Mix

In addition to the institutional stockholders who have reduced the average stock holding period to a mere nine months, there are two other stockholder groups worth examining. One has been around for some time while the other is relatively new to the scene.

The familiar are the venture capitalists. These are investors who typically supply equity capital at the early phases of a company's existence, The strategy of the venture capitalists is to take on the considerably greater risk of a start-up and earn above market average returns for assuming that risk. These are truly investors. Their mission is to actually supply funds to support the business strategy of the company they invest in. They provide cash.

In the Go-Go days of 1990s, the average annual return target for venture capitalists was as much as 35 percent a year. For the seven years from 1990 thru 1996, these investors actually earned more than 20 percent per year returns, compensating those investors with truly above market average returns. Since 1997, it has been a totally different story.

For the eight-year period beginning with 1998, the average annual return on venture capital investing has failed to meet investment objectives. The biggest annual loses occurred in the two reported years of 2004 and 2005.

The other major investor group in financial markets is relatively new. They are the private equity funds. These new investors act as intermediaries between the company and the general public of stockholders. They are pure human capital at work as they purchase the financial securities of the firm but do not invest in traditional fixed tangible assets. At the beginning of 2007, this group of investors were able to command a fee of 2 percent on assets under management and 20 percent of the profits earned, as Alan Murray of the Wall Street Journal described in the January 31, 2007 article. This has to be described as private equity management collecting hefty fees for what institutional stockholders used to do themselves, namely invest in companies rather than trade stocks. The controversy about private equity funds is around the use of financial leverage to buy the companies. Independent of the financial engineering used to actually complete the transaction and who provides the debt service and assumes the risk, private equity funds buy companies. Because they typically buy companies, they generally must hold the investment longer than the average nine months of institutional stockholders.

One must assume that institutional fund managers are bright motivated stockholders. To be paying the hefty fees to private equity funds, there must be some belief about higher returns that is motivating such behavior. One clue about this behavior is available from the comments the managers who run companies owned by private equity funds. In general, those managers sound like the managers of companies in the Berkshire Hathaway portfolio. What the managers of companies owned by private equity funds say is that, with the purchase by the private equity fund, the senior management is able to focus on a longer horizon to plan and execute business strategy. Put another way, by being out from under the pressure to produce ever higher quarterly earnings per share demanded by Wall Street, owners and managers feel they have the potential to create more value than if they worked for a publicly traded company. In the markets, this longer time horizon is commanding fees of 2 percent per year on assets and 20 percent of profits to warrant the investment shift from institutional fund stockholders to private equity investors. This is at least the *expected* incremental value of the private equity ownership otherwise the market would not pay the fees. Whether it is the actual incremental value of the private equity investors is yet to be seen.

Private equity funds are growing in importance in financial markets. When a single group of private equity investors buys a company it does so to take control. In general, these private equity funds act more like BH investors and less like stock traders. Recent evidence further affirms the trend.

Institutional investors are actually putting funds into private equity funds in an attempt to gain better returns. This is being done at a true economic cost in the form of the fees discussed earlier. This trend has caused many sophisticated observers to ask why this cost is being incurred. One explanation is that the institutional investors with an average holding period of .75 years are actually paying a fee to have an intermediary hold their investment capital for a longer period of time. This moves the investment further to the right on the time axis of figure 10.1. This is not the only movement to the right on the time axis taking place.

In a February 26, 2007 *Business Week* article titled "Hedge Funds Jump into Private Equity" (p. 46), the move away from the priority of the security analysts and toward that of Mr. Buffett was fully documented. "Most hedge funds require investors to keep their money locked up for a year. But funds moving into private equity are upping that period to three years."

One thing is clear. Hedge funds and private equity funds are acting very differently, with regard to holding period behavior than that exhibited by institutional stockholders and security analysts. Time will tell if the implicit move to a longer stock holding period, i.e., behaving more like investors than stock traders will produce better financial returns over the long run. The evidence indicates that a large group of investors believe that to be the case.

This second group of humans in the human capital investment picture split into two groups. On the one hand are the institutional stockholders influenced by the security analyst's framing of investment decisions. On the time line of investment holding period from figure 10.1, these "owners" act like the present is the timeframe for their decisions. They are pulled to the left of the time scale of investment decision making.

The other set of owners act much more like Mr. Buffett and the shareholders of Berkshire Hathaway. They are investors, owners who are willing to defer the temptation to act on the spur of the moment. They are much more willing to invest with a longer time horizon, one that includes the time required to develop strategy and retain the human capital of the enterprise.

The important thing about this group of humans in the human capital investment mix is how they behave when it comes to the issue of stockholder vs. investor behavior. Stockholder behavior responds much more to the priorities and framing of the security analysts who have a very short time horizon. At the other extreme are the investors like those who own Berkshire Hathaway, including Mr. buffett himself.

Recall that investment is the act of deferring current consumption to create greater value in the future. Given this role of time in investments, it is clear those humans located to the right on the time axis of figure 10.1 behave much more like investors than do mere stockholders. Investor behavior vs. stockholder behavior is important for both human capital decisions and the fixed tangible asset investments. Stockholders trade stocks.

In general, human capital assets take many years to create. It also takes years to develop highly productive leaders through the combination of education, training, and experience. This makes human capital itself a true investment.

In addition to the long time horizon required to develop human capital assets, these investments have both uncertainty of return and considerable risk to the "owners" of these assets, making them some of the least attractive investment alternatives for most stockholders from a risk point of view. The challenge is to produce measured returns and reduced risk as the means to increase the value created from human capital investments.

If there is one lesson learned from the data and analysis presented thus far, it is that one key to improved human capital investment decision making is to frame such decisions differently than is currently being done by the accountants and the security analysts.

14 The Challenge

American organizations spend a great deal on human capital investment. In 2006, American organizations spent more than $109 billion for education and training. The level of resources committed is confirmation of the executive belief that "our people are our most important asset." This conclusion is further supported by direct measurement. Seventy-five percent of surveyed chief executive officers stated that employee education is critical to enterprise success. That is a strong statement.

The executives spend the money for training and education. Yet only 14 percent of senior executive respondents described the overall skill level of their organization's entire workforce as industry leading. The anecdotal evidence indicates a poor return on a huge expenditure. But the real issue is whether the expenditures actually produce net favorable business impact. Little substantive analysis is being done to measure what is actually being procured for the one hundred and nine billion dollars being spent.

The expenditures are being made in spite of the fact that few measurements and even fewer analytical techniques have been developed to measure business impact produced from training and education expenditures. Also missing are measurements and methods to experiment and track changes in business outcomes over time. The irony is that the learning industry does not have the methods to learn about how to improve return and reduce risk over time.

An even bigger issue is whether the $109 billion, as large as it may be, is the right amount to be spending on human capital investment. Whether it should be less or more is an important strategic decision for companies and the nation. This is an increasingly critical issue in the face of the radically diminished importance of fixed tangible asset investments recorded on the balance sheet.

There is yet another factor that makes the level of investment in training and education a critical business issue. The theme of skills availability both today and in the future has risen dramatically in the eyes of American CEOs.

In the Business Council Survey of Chief Executive Officers dated February, 2007, the CEOs documented their concerns. On the question of finding qualified workers, the CEO response in 2006 was that about 25 percent of the surveyed CEOs said it was an issue. In the 2007 survey, that number expressing concern had risen to 43 percent. This is a near doubling in a little more than twelve months. The broader issue for CEOs is education in general.

The Business Council survey asked the question "how important are these policy issues to the United States?" The responses were rank ordered by percentage of CEOs calling the item important or most important. In the 2006 survey, education was ranked seventh. In the 2007 survey, education was ranked number one—above healthcare, energy, security, and tax policy. From this data, there can be no other conclusion than the one that human capital investment is viewed by senior level executives as critical. The challenge is to translate the general executive concern into a course of action, one that effectively directs expenditures to high yielding human capital investments.

Measurements and methods are required to make better human capital investments. In the absence of these critical management instruments, the effectiveness of investments in human capital is highly dependent upon the motivation and behavior of key humans who interact around the human capital issue. In the absence of good impact data and the related analyses, the one hundred and nine billion dollars being spent for training and education is being spent based on faith rather than analysis. The resources are being committed because senior leadership teams *believe* that people are their most important asset even though pitifully little data exists to select, evaluate, and validate that conclusion.

As a result, when earnings per share are threatened in an economic downturn, training and education are among the first expenditures to be cut. This incongruity between the mantra: "people are our most important asset" and executive actions leads to two disparate reactions. Security analysts praise the action while the employees impacted view the resulting fiscal cuts as violating the trust implied in the mantra. For the employees, skepticism is a natural reaction, one that undermines the loyalty of the employee over the long run.

The shift to managing humans as assets rather than only as expenses is more challenging than might at first be apparent. All of the current framing around the issues biases management prospective to expense over investment. Practical approaches to measuring future impact are key to the analyses needed to make better decisions.

15

Human Capital Supply—
A Call to Action

Over the next fifteen years, organizations will be sorely challenged to find an adequate supply of qualified people to compete. Over that period, more than seventy million of the most experienced workers in the US economy will be eligible for retirement. This is the number of the famous "Baby Boomer" generation who will reach retirement eligibility by early 2020. The raw number is staggering in magnitude, but alone it fails to fully capture the nature of the challenges that lie just over the horizon. The symptoms are already here.

A healthy world economy with steady growth creates demand for qualified workers. The demographics of the American work force defines the supply in the United States economy. The aggregate numbers are far too crude to fully reveal the details of the risks individual organizations face. The challenge for those organizations is to become informed about the global demographic trends and from that data, develop specific actions to protect their own competitive position in the global markets.

From the year 2000 until the year 2019, the critical population of twenty-five to forty-four year olds in the US economy does not growth at all. This particular segment of the US population includes the pool of emerging leaders—precisely the workers organizations want to develop into future leaders. This means that all organizations, both public and private, will be competing to recruit, develop, and retain workers in this critical population segment. The challenges are already being seen in the labor markets for qualified people.

Some have advocated outsourcing roles to other areas of the world economy. The outlook in the international community of developed nations is even grimmer than in the United States. Table 15.1 shows demographic data for the major international trading partners.

TABLE15.1
Changes in Population Ages 15 to 64 years Thru 2025

Germany	down 7 percent
Italy	down 14 percent
Japan	down 14 percent

Source: *The Economist*, "The Battle for Brainpower," October, 7, 2006, p. 4

Surprisingly, the talent shortage is not restricted to the mature economies of Western Europe and Japan. They exist in the emerging economies as well, especially in the economic power-houses of China and India. The nature of the talent shortage challenge in these countries is especially germane to the issues of education and investment cycles covered in this book.

In a well-researched piece appearing in Economist.com on April 16, 2007 titled: "Asia's Skill shortage: Capturing Talent," many of the supply issues are documented in detail. Among the major conclusions the *Economist* draws are the following specifics:

► A survey of 600 chief executives of multinational companies with business across Asia said a shortage of qualified staff ranked as their biggest concern in China. Given the specifics listed below, it is little wonder it is the number one concern of CEOs.
► The list of critical talent shortages spans many industries:
  ► India's shortfall in IT professionals by 2010 is 500,000;
  ► China will need many new business leaders. The current estimated stock is 3,000–5,000 and the need is 75,000 in the next ten years;

> ► China has 122,000 lawyers covering a population of 1,300 million compared to California's 192,000 covering a population 3 percent of China's size;
> ► China has 4,000 general practioner doctors and needs 160,000, to say nothing of the global shortage of nurses;
> ► India has fewer than 3,000 pilots today and will need 12,000 by 2025;
> ► China will need an average of 2,200 new pilots every year growing to 40,000 by 2025.

The specific supply issues and investment level challenges are very clear in the arena of the supply of pilots. Big international airlines are training a few hundred pilots a year. All of this in the face of the decline in the largest global population of pilots—those who fly for American carriers. Pilots flying for United States airlines must retire at sixty years of age. The dramatic decline in the supply of the most experienced pilots in the world is inevitable.

On top of these specifics, China has the same major structural problem that Western Europe and Japan has. The labor force in China will actually shrink over the next two decades. Like many demographic challenges today, the implications are completely counter intuitive. With the largest population in the world, the first intuition is that China and India have more than enough people to do virtually anything they want to do. What is missing from that conclusion is the fact that, for decades, China has had a one-baby policy. It takes more than two births a year just to replace the existing population in a nation. Even if China dramatically changes the one-baby policy today, the effects of the past decades still have a substantial impact on the critical 25- to 44-year-old population group explored in depth in the United States in chapter 15.

Supply of skilled, knowledgeable, experienced employees is a global issue. The development of the human capital required to create value in the twenty-first-century global economy is an investment that takes years to complete. The *Economist* article further sheds light on the recruiting vs. development issue.

What is especially interesting in the *Economist* analysis is the response that the emerging countries are taking to the pending talent supply—demand imbalance in the emerging economies. They are doing the same thing companies are doing here—they are "poaching" from each other. The inevitable results of this supply-demand imbalance are rapidly escalating wages and rising turnover. There can be no other outcome of a poaching strategy in the face of the global supply-demand imbalances.

The *Economist* article comes to exactly the same conclusion advanced here. The only solution is to increase the supply of skilled, knowledgeable, and experienced employees. This must be done through education. The divergence between the *Economist* and the author occurs when it comes to how such acceleration in education can take place.

For many in the education supply debate, the issue is one of public policy. This approach advocates that governments need to improve the quality and output quantity of the public education systems. That needs to be done, but it is not enough. For this author, the issue is not one of public policy, but one of individual company self-interest. Companies need to invest in their human capital as a matter of value creation and competitive advantage.

It is not only the macro numbers that create a sense of urgency for dealing with the limited supply. Industry-specific data reveals an even more chilling prognosis. A return to the oil and gas industry provides specific data.

The world's oil and gas supply starts with what the industry calls "up stream" production. Up stream activities include all of the geological, exploration, and development activities related to oil and gas reserves. It is a critically important industry even as the world struggles to diversify energy sources. The human capital needed to find and develop oil reserves takes a long time to develop. Education, training, and experience are all critical parts of the development of the industry's human capital.

The global up stream oil and gas industry faces the prospect that, by 2020, the industry will have lost 45 percent of the most experienced employees working in the industry in 2005. This represents a huge exodus of human assets, not only in the form of training and education, but in terms of knowledge gained from "on the job" experience. By 2020, the industry will be staffed with more than 50 percent of the work force thirty-five years of age and younger. The impact of this change is not only in terms of the investment required to develop the replacement human capital, it also has an impact on the productivity of the industry. Excellent research by experts at PetroSkills and J. M. Campbell published in the Journal of the Society of Petroleum Engineers analyzes the negative productivity from the loss of human capital knowledge and experience.

From the early 1970s to the early 1980s, the exploration and production portion of the global oil and gas industry had to hire and develop new inexperienced workers to meet the increased number of drilling rigs brought into service over that period. What the research shows is that there was a greater than 20 percent reduction in industry performance as measured by average feet per day drilled world wide. This 20 percent reduction in performance was shown to relate to the fact that more than 20 percent of the workforce had less than five years of industry experience. This lack of experience is precisely the situation that inevitably faces the industry in the next fifteen years.

From this data, it is clear that the threat from the retiring experienced work force extends far beyond the cost to hire replacements. The related danger is the reduction in productivity of the less experienced work force that replaces the experienced departing workers. This low productivity feature of new, inexperienced human capital is exactly the opposite of new fixed tangible asset investments. New fixed tangible asset investments bring the latest equipment technology into the acquiring organization. This brings better productivity with the investment because the new equipment is designed to include the latest know-how. So, in fixed tangible asset investments, the productivity improvement is high at the initial investment point and goes down over time from there.

Human capital is exactly the opposite. The new hires have a negative productivity impact upon initial hire and then, on average, their productivity increases over time making them more valuable in the future than at the time of the hiring. This is just one of the ways that human capital assets differ from capital assets on the balance sheet. A later chapter explores more of the contrasts to help managers frame their discussions about human capital investments using the characteristics of fixed tangible assets as a means to frame the issues.

One additional source of industry specific data, this one from the public sector, is valuable to examine. The US Department of Defense manages major procurement activity through a branch of the department called the Defense Acquisition Management Agency (DCMA). This agency is staffed by certified and experienced procurement professionals with at least a bachelor degree. Procurement certification and experience requirements for the profession range up to four years on the job. The data of importance is the comparison of the DCMA workforce with the general population.

In DCMA presentations, the data shows that the general population of baby boomers in the US labor force is 42 percent of the total population. That is a large number. At DCMA, the baby boomer population is 76 percent of the total, making it nearly twice as high a percentage as in the general population. Clearly, the agency has a human capital challenge every bit as great as the oil and gas industry.

The critical supply issues for the federal procurement and acquisition community extends well beyond DCMA. The broad issues have been building for a number of years and extend across the federal government. Some of the most successful organizations at recruiting and developing critical human capital are the various branches of the military. In the military human capital strategies, the offer to invest in the education of the young person being recruited is an important part of the recruiting efforts.

This industry specific data is critically important to developing a human capital strategy. It will be nearly impossible for an individual company to create and manage a human capital investment strategy without knowing the comparable data for their industry.

16

Developing vs. Recruiting

It is clear that time is central to the concept of investment and even more important in human capital investments. The distribution of the four groups of humans on the investment time continuum is shown in figure 10.1. That figure shows the four groups of humans relative to each other on the time axis. There is another dimension of time that is especially important to the discussion. That dimension involves the supply of human capital over the next fifteen years.

The senior management of organizations are playing a high stakes game of chicken with their human capital. Senior level executives have been hooked on the labor market supply-demand imbalance that existed in the first five years of the twenty-first century. As the US economy emerged from the tech bubble bust of 2000, labor markets were left with labor supply in excess relative to demand. During that period, the temptation had been to recruit new skills, knowledge, and experience rather than develop it.

The evidence of excess of supply over demand is in the data on real wages. Not until the latter part of 2006 did real wages begin to grow, indeed, for the prior five years of the twenty-first century the real wages actually declined. Declining prices are a sure sign of supply in excess of demand. Now pressures on wages are growing, and has become an inflation risk, as stated by the US Federal Reserve Board.

In a labor market with excess supply, recruiting was the preferred alternative for securing human capital. If companies needed new skills, they merely went into the market and purchased them. The recruiting bias remains even though the supply of skilled workers relative to demand is already becoming a factor. The survey of CEOs referenced earlier is just one of many. The Department of Labor reported job openings of four point two million in October, 2006, up 8.8 percent from a year earlier. This number is bound to do nothing but grow as the baby boomers actually begin to retire.

In the face of the compelling evidence and the certainty of the demographic trends in the next decade, the question one must ask is "why aren't companies more aggressively investing in their human capital?" The answer is related to the characteristics of recruiting vs. learning and development. There are a number of biases that favor the decision to recruit. Here are a few.

One important dimension is risk. When humans are viewed as the biggest expense on the income statement, the bias is to view human capital as excessive, leading to the conclusion that the enterprise has too many employees. Employees are the largest cost element on the income statement and the smallest entry (zero) on the balance sheet. Since human capital never appears on the balance sheet as an asset with future value, the bias has been to view humans only in the present and mostly framed as an expense. Thus the bias is to manage in a way that motivates managers to have fewer employees to avoid being "over staffed." Over staffing is particularly repugnant to security analysts who often celebrate when companies announce significant reductions in their work force.

A "just in time" approach to hiring similar to that used to manage inventory has been especially popular in recent years. When needed, the approach has been to crank up the human resource department to place ads, interview, and hire the talent and skills needed from the labor market. From about 2000 through 2005, that approach had been more than adequate to assure the talent, skills, and knowledge required to operate. A dramatic shift occurred in 2006. In 2006, real wages accelerated, causing concerns about labor cost impact on inflation. Both real market costs reflected a tightening labor market and survey data confirmed the conclusion. The beginning of the reversal of the supply-demand balance had begun. Demographic data confirms that the shift is certain to continue into the future.

There are only two options for having the talent, skills, knowledge, and experience required to compete in the future. A firm can either recruit it or it can develop it. Development has been the second choice behind recruiting partly because of the risk to the company associated with education. New policies, procedures, and practices to manage the risk while concurrently accelerating the level of investment is critical. Every executive can give multiple anecdotal examples where an employee was trained or received a degree, only to find out that the person turned out to be incapable of doing the expanded tasks even after the company investment had been made.

There is also the risk of departure. Many executives express, with conviction, that training, and especially education in the form of a bachelor or master's degree increase the likelihood that the employee will resign from the firm and move to a new opportunity. There is excellent research indicting that education can, in fact, be used as a retention tool when managed properly. Appendix D provides summaries from three research studies each documenting improved retention resulting from corporate investment in education.

Cost, risk, and retention related to recruiting vs. development are widely different. Far more is spent to recruit a single highly qualified new employee than is spent to train and educate an existing employee. On the risk side, expenditures to help an employee get an education are widely seen as unmanageable. Recommendations for reducing those risks are provided in detail in chapter 23. With regard to retention, the data shows that individuals recruited for a position have significantly higher departure rates than those promoted from within. One estimate is that as many as 50 percent of newly recruited MBAs depart their hiring firm within eighteen months of being hired.

Yet, even in the face of these facts, organizations are largely ambivalent when it comes to actually preparing for the dramatic shift in the supply-demand relationship that is inevitable in the next fifteen years. Many of the behaviors that served the senior level executives well in the past no longer serve the interest of the executives and the employees today. For most security analysts and many institutional stockholders, the ambivalence appears of little consequence in their value creation analysis.

One other factor works against companies aggressively investing to develop employees through education. Companies do not fully exploit the potential of universities as a means to develop high quality leaders. For the most part, there has been an arms-length relationship between companies and universities where universities are viewed by both as autonomous and independent. For decades the output of colleges and universities has been graduates with bachelor and master's degrees. The content of those degrees are largely dictated by the priorities of the universities. The degrees are the personal assets of the graduates who are then recruited by the companies. Under this recruiting approach, new skills and knowledge enter the company via the route of the new hire. With the historical emphasis on recruiting, many view the market for graduates as something that is a given. If one potential employee does not have the qualifications being sought, the response has been to interview another candidate. This worked fine when there were lots of candidates. That will not be the case in the near future.

The arms-length relationship between companies and universities has repressed collaborative relationships between companies and universities, especially in the area of curriculum development. Joint curriculum development between companies and universities has the potential to create new value. Measurement of business outcomes resulting from such customized curriculum has the potential to further increase the value created. The delivery of educational content that actually has value in the real world has a certain stench for academics at some traditional educational institutions. Nonetheless there are emerging educational innovators committed to collaboration. Among these is Bellevue University outside of Omaha, Nebraska.

The advice to both companies and universities is: "get over it." You need each other. For colleges and universities, the future supply of traditional high school graduates is grim. The number of high school graduates peaks in 2007 and declines for many years thereafter according to higher education sources.

The market for the traditional student is not a growth market. It is actually declining. Many universities need new markets to remain financially viable.

At the same time, companies need a significant increase in the supply of skills and knowledge to compete in the twenty-first-century global economy. Given the demographics over the next fifteen years, a significant increase in the total supply is needed. The only option is to increase the productivity of the work force through talent selection and investment to develop the improved skills and knowledge required to compete. The educational output must be more targeted, more efficient. In the face of fewer freshmen entering traditional programs, the best option is to increase the skills and knowledge with the employees the firm already has.

While the number of human bodies that will be available cannot be expanded, certainly their capacity to produce the required mental tasks is expandable. Companies need to approach their human capital with the same passion for productivity improvement that is a typical of productivity improvements sought from fixed tangible assets. It is the productivity of human capital that is the potential solution to the huge skills supply-demand mismatch looming up over the horizon. Human resource departments are in the position to lead the way to this solution.

17
Human Asset Value vs. Time

Retention is a term most often used in conjunction with recruiting as in: "recruiting and retention." The word association implies a natural link between the two—somewhat like bread and butter. Retention is almost never used in conjunction with development as in: "development and retention," even though development has far more impact on retention than does recruiting. Though spoken as the sequence recruiting and retention, the actual relationship between the two is retention and recruiting. The value relationship actually progresses from retention to recruiting. If the organization does not retain key employees, the organization is forced to recruit in order to replace the departed.

In the absence of successful retention policies, the impact is measured in terms of what it will cost to replace the departed employee(s). This frames retention as a current period expense. Thus, in this framing, the value proposition of retention is measured in terms of recruiting cost expenditures related to advertising, interviewing, and lost output while the position is vacant. These are the variable costs of replacing the departed employee. When retention is framed in the context of human capital and investment measurements, the approach is quite different.

The risk to the enterprise when human capital is managed as an asset is the value related to improved retention. Retention has an important time relationship to the actual value of the human asset for the company. The time value of the "human asset" is a combination of two independent factors that impact

97

the value of human assets over time. Advertisements to recruit new valuable employees often contain the following phrase:

"Bachelor degree and three to five years experience."

The degree represents the value of the formal education. Experience is a clear value enhancing element of human capital. Unlike fixed tangible assets, generally the passage of time actually increases the value of human assets.

The US Department of Labor states that 70 percent of the knowledge an employee gains is directly derived from experience on the job. But the increase in skills and knowledge is not gained instantaneously. It is gained over time. Thus, if we plot the relationship between time and the skills and knowledge gained from on the job experience, the result looks something like that shown represented in figure 17.1 where the skills and knowledge gained is represented as the human asset value on the Y axis.

FIGURE 17.1

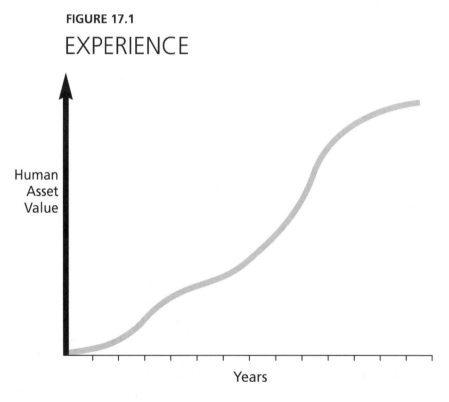

What the solid line represents is the increase of skills and knowledge over time from on-the-job experience. The line is not linear, but it is cumulative. Little is learned at first, but, over time, the employee's knowledge builds on itself, making new knowledge and skills more valuable after the building of an initial experience base.

The experience line is interesting for a number of reasons. For one, the skills and knowledge are gained without direct company cash expenditures. To put this another way, the company doesn't have to spend anything extra for this gain in human asset value. It is "free." It is a byproduct of the employees doing their job.

This is especially tempting to some because the company never has to report an expenditure of any extra cash to build the asset value. The cost never appears on the income statement. The fact that it is "free" makes it very tempting for managers to defend on-the-job training (OJT) as the primary, if not the only, development strategy of the firm. We will return to the implications of that strategy at the end of this chapter.

The solid line in figure 17.1 has several additional features important to human capital investment. The first attribute is that it increases over time and probably has positive slope for at least the first three to five years of employment (thus the specification in HR recruiting ads). This means that all employees are not equal in asset value. Some are more valuable than others.

Another attribute of figure 17.1 is the value of the experience gained relative to the type of experience gained. Figure 17.2 below is enhanced to include the experience of the company's employee experience vs. experience gained through employment in another industry. So the dotted line in figure 17.2 depicts the asset value of experience gained in a totally different industry. To see the relationship, think of the company represented in figure 17.2 as a pharmaceutical company and the solid line as experience gained working for that company. The dotted line represents the value *to* a pharmaceutical company from experience gained by an employee working for an oil exploration company.

Were the company represented in figure 17.2 an oil exploration company, the relative value of the experience represented by the dotted line and the solid line would be reversed. The point is that the asset value gained through experience (OJT) can be valued only relative to a specific firm in a specific industry, not as a general transferable asset from one company to all companies. While this may seem obvious, it has important implications for how retention is managed in organizations where people are valued as an asset.

FIGURE 17.2

INDUSTRY-SPECIFIC EXPERIENCE

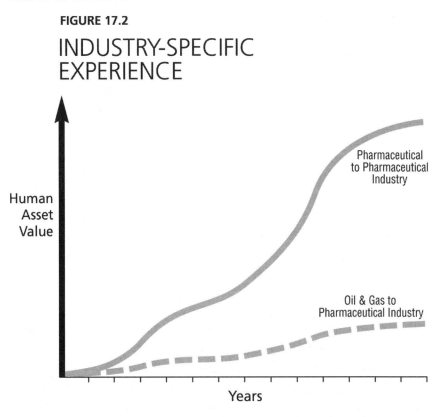

Figure 17.2 has competitive implications. The value of the experience gained by a company's employees is *most* valuable to other companies that are in the same markets, use similar language, have similar technology, and serve the same customers. That is, the value of accumulated experience is of greatest value to direct competitors of the firm. For this reason, direct competitors are willing to pay more to poach experienced employees because the recruitment of those employees adds the greatest immediate asset value to the firm doing the poaching.

FIGURE 17.3

RELATIVE VALUE OF EXPERIENCE

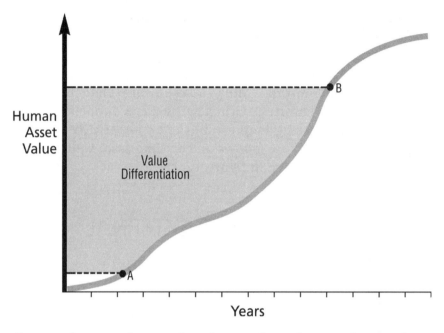

Conversely, it is obvious that the employee lost to the poaching competitor at point B in their career is greater than the loss of an employee at point A in their career. The total asset value loss is the difference of B minus A. This approach differentiates the value of employees in the same way that differentiating and segmenting customers is an important value enhancement activity for competitors. The gaming industry is one of the most sophisticated at segmenting its customers to maximize profit potential. In that industry, different groupings of customers are rigorously analyzed and provided differentiated services to increase total return.

In the outlook for the next fifteen years, the retiring baby boomers will be at point B on the curve in figure 17.3. Those with the greatest experience will be those departing. Those entering will be from a much smaller pool of less experienced individuals located closer to point A on the curve. This is especially the case when it comes to leadership skills and experience. This is the graphical representation of the oil and gas productivity analysis discussed earlier in chapter 15 where the negative impact was measured as a 20 percent reduction in productivity.

There is a second human asset value curve of importance to human capital investments. The single solid line shown in figure 17.1 is the accumulation of experience looked at from *within* the firm. There are value impacting forces that are at play from *outside* of the firm that must be considered. Outside the firm, the world is changing rapidly. New know-how is being created at mind-warping rates. Markets are changing. New competitors are entering with new business models. Global competition is altering long established competitive relationships. If we look at these factors on the time-asset value graph, the result is what we see in figure 17.4

FIGURE 17.4

EXPERIENCE PLUS EXTERNAL KNOW-HOW

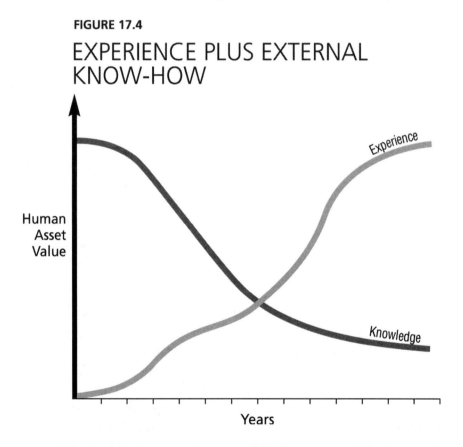

The knowledge line (declining) shows the effect of external know-how on the value of the human asset. If point one is the value of say a recent college graduate's education at the point in time when they get their degree and are hired by the firm, the knowledge line shows the value of that education in the future. The knowledge line represents the declining asset value of the recent graduate's education over time. In terms of the language of fixed tangible assets recorded by accountants on the balance sheet, the knowledge line shows the depreciated value of a formal education. The irony is that elaborate depreciation schedules exist for a huge number of fixed tangible asset classifications from trucks to buildings, yet no widely agreed upon standards to account for the depreciation of human assets exist.

Ironically, the most valuable human assets are actually the ones depreciating at the fastest rate as new know-how is being created. Salaries for recent graduates in new areas are highest at the time of hiring. Yet, over time, the education loses value rapidly as new developments increase the total body of knowledge.

With fixed tangible assets, the management requirements to remain competitive are well documented. When assets depreciate rapidly, as with computer hardware and software, an increase in the rate of replacement must take place to reinstate the value of the asset. Machinery rendered obsolete by new technology must be replaced by the latest equipment lest the firm lose ground in cost efficiency to more aggressive competitors.

There is another important implication of the knowledge line in figure 17.4. It is related to the development rate of new technology and innovation. Even if it's assumed that the experience line is in relatively the same position today as it was in, say, 1980, the knowledge line is not. In figure 17.5, we see a representation of the difference between 1980 and 2007.

What figure 17.5 represents is the impact of an accelerating rate of external knowledge creation. That acceleration has a very different impact on the net value of the human capital today than it did in the industrial production era as recently as the 1980s. When know-how was increasing at a relatively slow rate, the impact on the depreciating value of the know-how at the time of graduation was relatively minor over time, as represented

FIGURE 17.5

VALUE OF TRADITIONAL ACADEMIC DEGREE

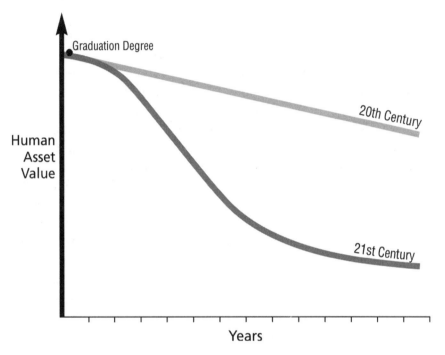

by the knowledge line in figure 17.4. It is likely that the aggregate result of experience gained on the job, combined with the loss of relevance of learned know-how from traditional degree programs, still resulted in a net gain in the human asset value, even without reinvestment in the humans of the organization. This means that the net value of the human assets increased over time independent of expenditures for training and education.

The resultant integration of the knowledge line and the experience line in figure 17.4 meant that the company could gain human asset value without committing cash or reducing current period reported earnings by an exclusive recruiting of new graduates human capital strategy. This made on-the-job training (OJT) a preferred avenue—a bias that remains at some companies to this day.

The problem for companies in the twenty-first-century global economy is that the knowledge line in figure 17.4 no longer applies. The half life of knowledge is rapidly decreasing. Or, put another way, the rate at which new knowledge is being created is accelerating. The result is that the value of the original knowledge obtained through formal education at the beginning of one's career is depreciating more rapidly. The knowledge gained by the traditional twenty-two year old graduating from a university rapidly becomes obsolete in the absence of more aggressive reinvestment. What is really occurring is more accurately reflected in figure 17.6 where the twenty-first century know-how line shows the impact of rapid external knowledge development.

FIGURE 17.6

EXPERIENCE

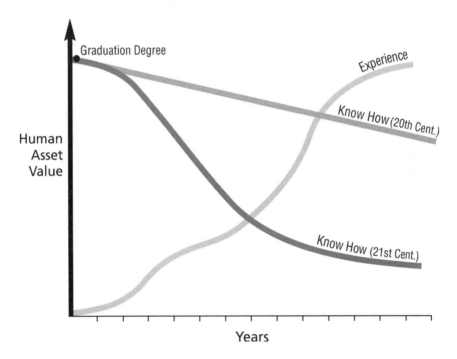

When the depreciated knowledge value of the traditional formal education is combined with the increased value gained from experience, the net impact on the value of the human capital is very different than in the past. In the industrial production era, the combination of depreciation of human capital assets from external know- how and experience gained over time likely had a net positive impact on the human asset value. In today's world, the net result might, at best, be the status quo or even declining human asset value over time. Understanding this result is an important issue for human capital investment decision making.

Unlike the case with fixed tangible assets on the balance sheet, the impact of the passage of time on the value of the human asset probably increases with time rather than decreases. This makes retention all the more critical. The second implication is that, even with increasing experience, the value of the knowledge a twenty-two year old possesses upon graduation has nothing to do with how long they are with one company or another. The new knowledge being created is outside of their own firm and goes on independently of the work experience gained within the firm. In the absence of continued reinvestment to bring the new knowledge from outside the firm into the human capital asset base, the net value of the formal knowledge depreciates and, in the twenty-first-century global economy, it depreciates at an accelerating rate.

To enhance or even preserve the value of the human assets, reinvestment in skills and knowledge must take place over time. Without reinvesting, the knowledge component, the 30 percent not gained through OJT, certainly depreciated and it may be the case that the net of the two declines over time. The issue, then, is not whether the organization should reinvest in its human capital. It must. The issue is *at what rate* should that reinvestment take place?

18

Human vs. Tangible Assets—
Value Divergence

I t has been asserted that humans cannot be *managed* as assets because GAAP accounting rules do not allow the *reporting* of expenditures for training and education as assets on the balance sheet. Companies strictly follow GAAP principles, and those same rules frame the way decision makers think about human capital investments.

Some have argued that, because GAAP rules do not allow accounting for expenditures on training and education as entries on the balance sheet, they should not be managed as investments. This framing blocks the viewing of training and education expenditures as assets that create measurable future value. Such an approach fails to deal with the risks and time profile of returns related to such investments. Examination of how balance sheet assets are actually managed in the value creation activity is revealing.

When completed, a new building is recorded at historical cost as a fixed tangible asset on the balance sheet. From that day forward, the recorded value of that fixed tangible asset declines as a result of booked depreciation. On the balance sheet of the company, the net value of the building over time looks like the line in figure 18.1.

Although the net fixed tangible asset value declines over time according to GAAP accounting rules, the true economic value may go in the opposite direction. The *market* value of the asset may actually be increasing over time, but the GAAP rules do not allow the company to account for increasing market value

FIGURE 18.1

ACCOUNTING FOR A BUILDING

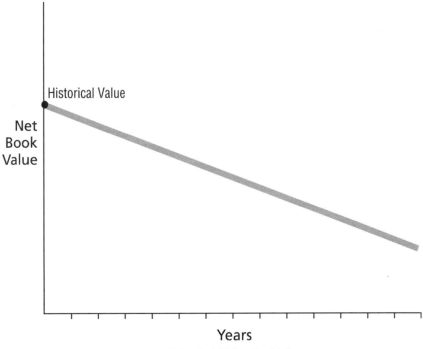

Note: straight line depriciation

on the balance sheet. Even though the accounting rules don't allow the market value of the asset to be booked, most business decisions are made to manage the asset relative to market value, not relative to book value. The gain or return from the appreciated market value is the actual value path even though GAAP does not account for that value on the balance sheet. The market value is realized only when the building is actually sold. With human capital assets, the assets are never sold and therefore, under GAAP rules, cannot be restated, even in the future.

The clearest example of a value creation case is a commercial real estate company that builds commercial property in an area where growth is occurring. The decision to make the initial investment is based entirely on the outlook for the future. The point is that economic value is based on external forces over time. The future is crucial to the value creation.

The building is financed and built on the current costs reflected on the balance sheet of the company and the loan statement of the bank financing the project. In reality the entire project is built under the expectation that external market forces will increase the market value of the asset being built along with the rental cash flow even while the balance sheet net asset value is continuously declining.

In the value creation process of the building, the investors are actually making expenditure decisions on the basis of the market value forecast that is never reflected on the balance sheet. The value creation resulting from the appreciation in market value works outside of the GAAP accounting rules. The net result of this value relationship is shown in figure 18.2

FIGURE 18.2

BUILDING MARKET

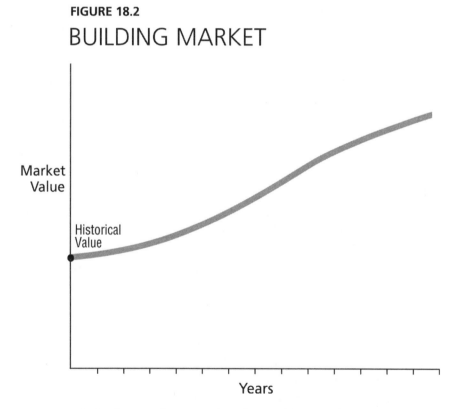

Figure 18.2 shows that, under favorable market conditions, external market forces not shown on the balance sheet offset the depreciating book value of the asset shown on the balance sheet.

The net result is that the executives of this firm make decisions about return and risk to create value *independently* of the fact that the true value drivers impacting their decisions are not reported in the official financial statements. The skill with which the investors understand the value creation factors in their markets determines the return they produce on their investment. Those returns have little to do with the historical cost figures entered on the balance sheet.

Similar factors apply to investments in human capital as apply to the building value financed by the commercial developer. The GAAP accounting rules for entry on the balance sheet have little to do with value creation over time of the investment being made.

The one advantage the commercial real estate developer has over the human capital investment case is access to external financing based on recorded asset value. The rules of banking allow the commercial real estate developer to leverage the investment by borrowing investment capital from the bank. The amount of those potential borrowings are determined by the book value shown on the balance sheet as well as the *forecasted future* cash flow to service the debt. No such leveraging of asset value is available to free cash for training and education investments.

One other interesting contrast between fixed tangible assets such as buildings booked on the balance sheet and human capital is what happens to the value of those assets over time. In the case of the building, time erodes the value of the booked net value of the asset, i.e., it declines over time. In the case of human assets, experience increases the value of the human asset. The contrast can be seen by comparing figure 18.1 with figure 17.1.

If we go back and look at retention as the act of keeping the asset, the comparison between the building and the humans has exactly opposite value implications. In the case of the humans, departure of a person early in their tenure with the firm represents minimal lost value for the firm. In this case, the departing employee has little experience; therefore, not much is at risk other than the loss of the firm's cost to recruit them in the first place.

Exactly the opposite is the case for the building. Loss of the building in the first year after construction represents the greatest loss of asset value in terms of net book value and value to the bank used for lending purposes. Over time, the building becomes *less* valuable while the human assets become *more* valuable. Because asset retention issues are framed by executive decisions about fixed tangible assets like buildings, the divergence of value over time has not generally been considered. This also may be one explanation for why retention is not typically viewed as a strategic issue for the company. At the same time, this increase in human capital value over time is another reason it is critical to manage humans as capital assets of the firm—assets with increasing value. The strategic challenge is to invest in training and education to make those assets even more valuable in the future by offsetting the depreciation of the knowledge present at the time of graduation from a university.

While GAAP accounting principles are important for assuring objectivity of investment data, it is not one of the necessary factors in management decisions for creating value from investments, either tangible and intangible. It is the quality of the management policies, practices, and procedures used to make allocation decisions that determines the value created, not whether the result of the decision is recorded on the balance sheet.

19
Investment in Intangibles

The data and conclusions in chapter 1 show that in the twenty-first century, investments in assets on the balance sheet are *not* creating the majority of the growth in value as measured by: stock market price, productivity, GDP, and corporate profits. This helps senior level executives focus on more value creating investment alternatives among the intangible assets of the firm. As important as this is, it does not define what intangibles to invest in and, more importantly, how to measure the return on those investments to improve the total value created over time.

Better measurement of the return on intangible assets helps executives compare and assess investment alternatives across the full spectrum of tangible and intangible assets. Of equal if not greater importance is the need to define new, previously unidentified investment alternatives. Measurements combined with analysis helps decision makers learn over time. A human capital example reveals the case.

In the book, *ROI on Human Capital Investment*, the return on investment from earning a bachelor degree in the United States economy is derived for both the individual and, in the case where the company funds all or a part of the education through tuition reimbursement, the return for the company. The main conclusion is that, based on the rate of return, an investment in an accredited degree in the American economy is a "no brainer" for the employee. The conclusion is overwhelmingly confirmed by the financial calculations. What is also confirmed is that, with policies and procedures designed to maximize retention, the company also has a very favorable return *even accounting for the risk that the employee might resign after getting their degree.*

For the individual, the investment decision is rather simple. The employee can either decide to invest in an education or not. Basically, it is a zero or one decision. But even where the decision is fairly straightforward, the return calculation reduces the uncertainty resulting from the decision. The real opportunity for better investment decision making is with the data and related analysis. The individuals can significantly increase their return on investment through related career choices. Among these is the decision to join a firm that has a generous tuition assistance program as part of the company benefit package. This recruiting rationale is the one most often made by human resources managers to defend the education benefit even though it is accounted for as an expense to operations. What is missing in most company decision processes are the measurements required to create even greater value.

As the war for talent heats up over the next fifteen years, it will be important for companies to use every resource available to be the successful competitor in the war to attract *and* retain the talent, skills, and knowledge required to compete in end markets. Under this future scenario, it is critical that the education benefit be used to the maximum potential to both recruit and retain talent.

When it comes to the importance of the education to the company, there are only two outcomes possible. Either the tuition reimbursement benefit does indeed assist in recruiting as the human resources department asserts or it does not. In either case, the company should be doing the data gathering and analysis to understand how to get a better return on the investment.

In the case that the tuition assistance benefit is not assisting in the recruiting of new talent the benefit should be discontinued in the absence of some other rationale for the expenditure (investment). If the tuition assistance expenditure helps recruiting, then the company should aggressively promote the benefit rather than tepidly offering it as is currently being done at many companies.

The problem is that the overwhelming majority of companies have no concrete measurements to assess whether the benefit actually does what it is purported to do with regard to recruiting. The important issue for the senior management team is not whether the benefit should exist but whether the company should be more aggressively investing as a strategy in the talent war or eliminating the budget item altogether as a cost saving. The point is that the gathering of the data and the related analyses are not the end point of the effort. Merely seeking to justify what already exits does not significantly contribute to the value creation process. The return analysis is a basic building block for understanding and defining *what should be done differently in the future.*

For the company, the potential to learn and create new practices that improve the ROI on the educational investment is even greater. The employee in human capital investment interjects free will into the investment equation. A disciplined measurement and modeling approach has even greater implications for the company by providing feedback on other personnel parameters such as promotion, supervisor training, and the impact of salary actions, to name a few. By having the measurements to evaluate and prioritize measured results, the company can experiment and innovate. What will be critical to the rapidly changing world of the future is the practice of experimentation and measurement to learn what to do even better the next time. Because turnover is the risk parameter in the human capital investment decision, the impact of learning over time has multiple implications.

In both *ROI on Human Capital Investment* and the companion work *Competitive Advantage from Human Capital Investment*, the impact of both salary actions and promotions on retention are explored. The implications of these two key company activities are worth analysis.

Salary increases and promotions are important to the employee from an income perspective. More money is good. More money buys more things. More money reduces personal risk in an uncertain world. More money creates more life options. But money is not everything. In fact, among the X generation, money is ranked very low as a motivator. What then is the critical insight related to money and the issue of return on human capital investments?

The answer is that money sends a signal. It is a strong statement to the employees who have earned a degree that they are more valuable than they were previously. The commitment of their time, energy, and, in many cases, their own money was indeed a good investment. They see themselves as valuable assets to the company. This linkage is related to motivation and behavior and not solely to economic outcome.

As a result of switching costs (see appendix C) and the motivational factors involved, the company does not have to hand over the total increase in market value from a degree just earned. As a result of switching costs, the company can capture the lion's share of the added value. But the human resources department must have a strategy to take advantage of the links between new skills and knowledge and personnel issues such as salary and promotion.

Since there is very little good data on exactly how much salary increase is required to significantly impact retention, the challenge for senior leadership is to try some salary action and measure the impact. Experiment and learn over time.

Why is it so important to deploy actions targeted at learning when it comes to intangible investments? We have already established that the significant growth in value is being created by intangible assets, not tangible assets. The second reason is because we know so little about how to make good intangible asset investments, especially when it comes to human capital where the wild cards of motivation and behavior intercede between capital allocations and desired business outcomes.

When it comes to the linkage between salary actions and retention, we are operating in an area of knowing between the last and the next to last lines in table 19.1.

TABLE 19.1
The Three Levels of Knowing
We know what we know.
We know what we don't know.
We don't know what we don't know.

Humans are most comfortable making decisions where the first two cases apply—when we know what we know and we know what we don't know. While sometimes uncomfortable, venturing into the domain of "we don't know what we don't know" is often the most productive of the three domains of knowing. We are close to the latter when it comes to data on the linkage between salary and motivation of employees related to the awarding of an accredited degree.

20 The Known and the Unknown

I n tangible asset investments, we know that we know a great deal about how to measure and analyze financial return from the various tangible asset investments based on a century of financial modeling developed during the industrial production era. Here are a few things that are known about tangible asset investing.

It is known that, for a hundred years, the assets that created value were those on the balance sheet. These were the assets that were required to produce the things people demanded in end markets. That was the era when things like machines were required to produce more things like automobiles, washing machines, desks, and more machines to name a few. This was the grand era of manufacturing. In this era, the human was subservient to the machine. This was the era when skills were deployed in the form of very specific training dictated by the characteristics of the fixed tangible assets. The production machines defined what training was necessary and what training created value.

The specific training needed during the industrial production era was largely defined by the form and technology of the tangible asset producing the output. When printing presses were indeed presses that printed, typesetting was a valuable skill. The form of the skill and the related value proposition was dictated by the operations and technology of the presses being used. Changes in printing technology dictated changes in the training required to operate the machines. As soon as mechanical typesetting was invented, the value of human typesetting

119

skills plummeted, a cycle that was to be repeated again when mechanical typesetting was displaced by electronic word processing and laser printers in today's information age. The point is, we know that the value of skills during the industrial production era was dictated by the output value of the tangible asset requiring the skill to operate it.

Another important thing that we know about the value of skills during the industrial production era was that the GAAP principles were more than adequate to assign a value to the tangible asset. The assignment of historical costs to the value measurement represented minimal risk to decision makers. The risk was low because markets and technology were both changing at a relatively slow rate. In addition, traditional competitors were relatively stable and easily observable. The important competitors were the companies with the assets similar to those you had and value could be assigned to outputs by counting the number of things that came off of the end of the assembly line.

We also knew what we didn't know. We knew that we could not forecast the future price of a barrel of crude oil and therefore could not assign a market value to the hydrocarbon reserves of an oil field—a decision accountants made some time ago. But not knowing didn't matter very much. For decades, the price of a barrel of crude oil was relatively low and changed at a reasonably measured pace, at least until the 1970s. Stable global geopolitics reduced the risk to supply. No country in the Middle East posed a threat to the safety and security of the oil fields. We knew we did not know how the use and price of oil would change in the future, but little was at risk as a result of that uncertainty.

What we did not know was that all of that would change within our lifetimes. Stable oil sources came under increased threat of disruption. The result has been volatility in end markets. Sharp and painful price spikes in oil have rippled through the global economy.

Late in the twentieth century, we did not know how pervasive the impact of information technology would be on our lives. But not knowing what we did not know did not limit the use of the phrase: "the information age," even though we had no idea of the true implications when the particulars were put to practice. What we did not know we did not know was that the assets so important to the industrial production era, those on the balance sheet, would fade in importance in the twenty-first-century global economy. That transition took only about twenty-five years to happen and only now are the true implications becoming clear.

What lies before us is the great expanse of unknown and unmeasured intangibles. Intangible assets are those that lie in the territory of a huge unexplored wilderness, not unlike the great western regions of North America before Mr. Merriweather Lewis and his fellow adventurers explored the west in the early nineteenth century. In the early 1800s, the great Lewis and Clark expedition bravely stepped forward, fully aware that there was a huge expanse that held mysteries beyond the imaginations of that era. Those explorers freely admitted that they did not know what they did not know. What empowered them was their courage to admit the state of their knowledge about the territory they were exploring. Today we are in a similar position when it comes to investments that create value in the twenty-first-century global economy.

The massive distribution of cash in the form of common stock buybacks is an admission by corporate leaders that good investment alternatives are difficult to identify. Also clear is that intangibles are more important than tangible assets in the creation of new value in the twenty-first-century global economy. In no domain is this more true than that of human capital investments.

21

Barriers to Increased Value Creation from Human Capital Investments

The potential for significant competitive advantage resides in the policies and procedures of the human resources (HR) department. Those policies are largely driven by industrial era value structures focused on cost control and compliance. Both cost control and compliance remain important drivers for training; however, new strategic opportunities exist—opportunities catalyzed by the view of human capital and investment as in "our people—our most important asset."

One of the dominant characteristics of existing HR policies is the company-wide nature of the procedures used to enforce them, particularly in the areas of compensation and benefits. The organization does not want to be exposed to uncontrollable compensation and benefits costs that vary from department to department. Allowing the biggest cost element of operations to be subject to the whims of individual operating managers is unacceptable. By creating job classifications with pay ranges, changes in cost structure are driven by promotions and not by individual negotiations.

The same rationale exists for company-wide benefits related to the job classification. Health benefits are tied to objective parameters and classifications. Pension benefits (where they still exist) are defined based upon salary level and longevity of employment. Tuition reimbursement policies are most often defined company-wide with procedures in place to cap total expenditures. Many of these uniform characteristics of HR policies and procedures have historical precedent as "best practices" widely accepted by the HR profession. Most of this historical precedent for uniformity is driven by the need to control the people costs of business operations. Under that scenario, the focus is on the income statement.

In recent decades, new external forces emerged that impact the management of HR policies and procedures. Not completely the result of political correctness, it is valid to recognize that these new forces relate more to political and moral factors than they relate to economic forces. Most of these new forces run counter to the motivation to control costs. One of the more predominant of these is compliance with requirements of the Equal Employment Opportunity Commission (EEOC).

While the title clearly states "Equal Employment Opportunity" many times the practice should more accurately be titled "Equal Employment Outcome." Fear of litigation bludgeoned leaders of many organizations to manage to outcomes as a way to manage risk. Whether this is in fact the route the organization chooses to manage risk in this area is the choice of the senior executives of the organization. The main point to be made is that it should be a choice, not a default operating outcome resulting from a failure to consciously select the level of risk the organization is willing to take.

In the twenty-first-century global economy, forces require the reexamination of monolithic policies, procedures, and practices. Competitive advantage from human capital investment requires that priorities be set for the allocation of expenditures in training and education. The National Bureau of Economic research shows that productivity is driven largely by investments in intangible assets, including people. "The fraction of output growth per hour attributable to the old "bricks & mortar" forms of capital investment is very small, accounting for less than 8 percent of the total growth for the period 1995–2003" (NBER research paper).

The entire approach of looking at investments in human capital as investment rather than current period expenses redefines many of the priorities for allocating resources. Practices long used in tangible asset allocation decisions form a starting point for innovation.

Prioritizing and selectively targeting investments in brick and mortar investment alternatives is never questioned when those priorities are set. As absurd as the comparison may seem, consider the fact that no external governing body questions when the senior executive team decides to build an office complex in one locale over another. The point is that tangible asset investment decisions such as buildings and equipment are made on a prioritized basis. For the most part, such resource allocation decisions are made using economic criteria, the most common of which is return on investment (ROI).

In the industrial production era, when tangible assets were the primary factors of value creation, use of ROI calculations for prioritizing investment alternatives was not questioned. The executives were chartered to make such prioritized decisions. It was a management responsibility to expend resources for some tangible assets while in turn not expending resources for other tangible assets. It is the act of not expending in other areas that is most important in this discussion of human capital investment.

Current HR policies and procedures are often enforced to avoid the "not choice" among the human resources of the organization. Benefits designed to be implemented company-wide take on a life of their own. Any hint that an education or training alternative is available to some employees but not to others, based on investment criterion is strongly resisted in HR departments. It will remain so as long as funding of education is viewed as an employee benefit rather than a company investment.

The basic practice being advanced in the HR discussion is that training and education expenditures should be prioritized. To be specific, some areas of the business should receive more human capital investment while other areas of the business should receive less investment based upon the characteristics of the skills and knowledge needed by the business. Equal opportunity to be eligible for the investment fund must be preserved. By implication, this means that some employees of the company might receive more investment capital to develop skills and knowledge while other employees might receive less. The EEO commission is chartered to enforce access to opportunity, not outcome.

22 Winning the War for Talent

Generals tend to fight the last war. In the case of turnover, the generals are not only the human resource managers, they are also the operating managers to whom employees report. In this case, the last war was all about the pay—a carpet bombing approach that flies in under the radar as just "show me the money." One of the themes advanced here is that the talent war of the future is about much more than money. It is about targeting the specific outcomes required to win. It is about identifying the laser bombs that go directly to the high value targets of the "talent war." Our goal is to equip the reader with some of those laser guided policies, procedures, and practices. To take full advantage of the potential, executives will need to experiment and evaluate the results. Data evaluation is required. There is no formula, no game plan that exists today.

The first thing we have to examine is exactly what is the talent war and why is it important to win it? The talent war is really about successfully competing for the talent, skills, and knowledge the organization must have to compete in the global economy of the twenty-first century. It is about having all of the dimensions of skills, knowledge, talent, and experience—the elements that constitute the human capital of the organization. The laser targeting begins by clearly distinguishing between talents, skills, and knowledge. The laser policies, procedures, and practices for a winning the high value targets for talents, skills, and knowledge are different. The goal is to *have* the human capital required. The distinction is that doing is not the same as having.

One carpet bombing approach is to allow turnover to be whatever it is going to be and simply adopt a strategy to recruit and replace those departed. This model accepts turnover as an uncontrolled variable—a given in the talent war. Such a strategy might have been successful when the supply of talent, skills, and knowledge was abundantly available in the labor markets. Skilled labor was abundantly available after the dot.com bust between 2000 and the end of 2005. The stagnation of real wage growth during the period is evidence of abundant supply. There were lots of bodies to be recruited, especially among the bulging population of baby boomers.

By mid 2006, real wages began to increase in US labor markets. The wage data confirmed the anecdotal evidence that there is a growing shortage of the skills and knowledge demanded by companies in the global economy. Given the demographics of the United States, indeed the world, the supply outlook becomes grimmer with each passing year. It will get worse over the next fifteen years as baby boomers retire, taking their skills, knowledge, and experience with them. A gaping hole in the supply will appear within the next few years with a smaller population of emerging leaders available to fill the gap. The key population is the group of eligible workers in the twenty-five to forty-four year old age group. Companies will face escalating real wages at best, and, at worst, there is a very real possibility that they will not be able to get, at any price, the talent, skills, and knowledge required to compete. The counterpoint to this last argument is that one can get anything with enough money. This may be true, but in the rapidly changing global economy, the issue is not whether one has enough money, but whether management is willing to spend the money *in time* to win.

Retention has to be one of the targets of choice for the laser policies and practices of the winners. Very simply, the specifications for the laser practices and the high value targets are those factors that improve retention. The industrial production era strategy of throwing money at the problem is way down the target list for the twenty-first century.

The first and most important target for improving retention is to understand why people leave organizations. Of equal importance is knowing what motivates others stay. The laser guidance needed here is to decrease the former while increasing the latter. These two factors are not mirror images of each other. Targeting requires a more refined approach.

Research shows that the number one issue that motivates people to quit their current job is the behavior of their immediate boss. People join companies, but quit bosses. Ironically, an excellent company brand helps recruiting, but does little for improving retention. It is not the pay, not the president of the company, not the earnings of the company that are critical to retention. It is the management skill of the employee's boss. Employees leave because their immediate supervisor behaves in ways that are not compatible with the motives of the employee.

Communication is an important supervisory skill. As a result, the first laser practice to be added to the arsenal of the talent war is to improve the leadership knowledge and skills of managers at all levels of the organization.

One huge mistake organizations make is to delude themselves about where the skills and knowledge to manage people actually comes from. The Labor Department estimates that as much as 70 percent of the knowledge required to do a job comes from the experience gained by doing the job itself. There are two problems with this carpet bombing approach to developing better managers. The first is that this makes the development of a good manager a process of trial and error. In such experiments, the employees reporting to the manager learning through on-the-job training are the lab animals of the experiment. The second problem with this approach is that, even if the learning manager gets the 70 percent from experience exactly right (and by this we mean gets the management skills and knowledge, but does so without causing significant employee resignations), there remains the 30 percent of the skills and knowledge that cannot be gained from OJT.

The 30 percent of the skills and knowledge required to be a good manager come from outside of the organization. This is the laser approach human resource and learning managers call "best practices." Among best practices are the successful deployment of such tools such as project management, learning management systems, "soft people skills" and Six Sigma. It is also the leadership skills needed to build and lead a high impact team.

Leaders are in short supply and much coveted by today's organizations. In the war for talent, "leaders" are those who can think critically, analyze complex data, synthesize divergent evidence in a coherent plan of action, define a vision and mission for the team, negotiate and resolve conflict and successfully communicate all of these upward and downward in their organizations. In the flat organizations of today, leaders are required at all levels of the organization. With these leadership skills and knowledge, the managers have a significantly higher probability of increasing the retention of their key human capital assets.

Successful targeting of retention as a strategic outcome requires more. A key element is the distinction between yesterday's work force and tomorrow's work force. What motivates our children is not what motivated our fathers. The next generation of leaders are different, and we will live and manage in that different era in the future.

The activities that motivate the next generation of employees are very different than those that motivated the retiring baby boomers. In an extensive survey of more than fifteen hundred people labeled Gen-X (which is the generation in that shrinking twenty-five to forty-four year old age group today), the mother-daughter authors of the book *The NeXt Revolution* present some very important data. In that survey, the authors asked those sampled to rank fifteen job characteristics important to them in their work. The contrast between the motivations of the prior leaders and those of the emerging leaders could not be more dramatic. The differences are critical to fighting the next war for talent.

Where most baby boomers identify salary, recognition, and job status as important motivators, these same factors ranked by the Gen Xers surveyed as near or at the very bottom of fifteen job characteristics important to them. The clear message from this portion of the survey is that, when it comes to motivators, targeting what worked in the past will be a pitfall of the future managers. It is fighting the last war.

The laser policies, procedures, and practices that will impact the X generation are identified in *The NeXt Revolution*. These are: Number one—positive relationship with their supervisor! This is yet another confirmation that it is the skills and knowledge of the direct supervisor that most impacts retention. Relationship with coworkers is important, and interesting work is also among the top four motivational items for that generation.

The fourth item of importance to the future leaders is "the opportunity to learn." This is also one of the factors The Gallup Organization measures with its Q-12 engagement instrument. The interesting thing about the opportunity to learn is that, by investing resources in education and training, organizations have the opportunity to create better managers while simultaneously improving retention. The investment in learning and education is a laser practice with a double impact—a kind of "two for" that further enhances the return on the human capital investment.

One characteristic of the last war on turnover is the myth that, by investing in an employee's education, especially accredited bachelor and master's degrees, the organization actually increases the likelihood of turnover. The myth is most often based on anecdotal evidence. With effective policies, procedures, and practices, education can be used to increase retention. Detailed evidence on the positive impact of education on retention is presented in appendix D.

One important laser guided practice needs to be shared here. This gem is targeted at the human resource and learning managers in the audience. When confronted with the recommendation that the organization communicate what skills and knowledge will be valuable to the company in the future, most HR managers refuse to take a stand. Such communications have a long list of potentially positive results for both the company and the individual employee. In the first place, the communication helps the employees target their own learning. By knowing what has potential value to the company, the employees can target their personal resources, namely their time, emotions, and intellectual energy to learning alternatives that have higher potential value rather than picking alternatives out of ignorance.

By communicating what the senior leadership sees as important future human capital needs, the leadership is providing the employee with a high target of opportunity for their personal learning investment. This is laser targeting in action. These actions increase the probability that the employee will be more valuable in the future while simultaneously improving the likelihood that the company will have the human capital it needs, all the while increasing the retention of the employee because they are more valuable to the firm in the future.

What often actually happens is that senior managers (in particular senior human resource leaders) are reluctant to communicate such a prioritized message to employees. One can only surmise that this behavior is out of a fear that providing guidance—by prioritizing the importance of some skills and knowledge over others, the organization will be expected to automatically compensate those who follow the guidance. In reality, there need be no Quid Pro Quo for the information. It is merely information that has the potential to help everyone make better human capital investment decisions.

When silence about what the leaders see for the future is the dominant form of current communications the result is to have a near random selection of learning alternatives. It is carpet bombing of human capital investments at its finest, both on the part of the company and as well as on part of the employee. It is a strategy of hope that something of value will be produced in the process. Give employees the laser! Let them target to everyone's benefit.

To the generals of the talent war, the advice is the same. The sophistication of precision policies, procedures, and practices has increased immensely not only in real warfare, but in the talent wars as well. The winners will be the ones with the most laser bombs to hit those high value targets—the ones that not only reduce turnover but, at the same time, increase the overall value of the organization's human capital.

23
Human Capital Investment vs. Capital Investment

The accounting profession disallows the recording of human capital investments as assets on the balance sheet because the enterprise does not have complete control of the asset. The human in the investment has control over the disposition of the asset. If the employee leaves the investing company, the value of the asset created immediately drops to zero for the departed company, rendering the original investment worthless. Worse yet, the asset often becomes valuable to a direct competitor.

The risk-return structure for employees is misaligned with the risk-return structure for the company when it comes to education. As a result of this misalignment, corporate leaders are reluctant to aggressively promote education as a human capital investment strategy.

Human Capital investment is defined by three activities.

1. *Education* provided by an accredited University with academic credits awarded toward a bachelor, masters, or Ph. D. degree.

2. *Training* delivered from an internal company source or nonaccredited third-party vendor (SkillSoft is an example).

3. *Experience* gained through performing tasks on the job.

Each of these activities has its own risk-return profile.

FIGURE 23.1

RETURN–RISK
Employee / Employer

	RISK	RETURN
EDUCATION	Employee: Low	Employee: High
	Employer: High	Employer: High
TRAINING	Employee: Low-moderate	Employee: Unknown
	Employer: Low-moderate	Employer: Not measured
EXPERIENCE	Employee: Low	Employee: Increasing over time
	Employer: Moderate over time	Employer: Increasing over time

The employee-employer comparisons shown in figure 23.1 reveals opportunity to enhance the value creation process. Both the employer and the employee have the same interests with regard to education. Currently, labor markets are screaming for more qualified candidates with higher levels of education. The high tech industry needs more engineers and, during the immigration bill debates in the summer of 2007, lobbied Congress to expand the H1B program.

In the American economy, the value of a bachelor degree over no degree is more than twenty thousand dollars per year in income over the working life of the employee. And the additional income value of a master's degree over a bachelor degree is approximately the same differential. These prices confirm that education creates incremental value for employers who are willing to pay a premium for those levels of education in the labor markets. If expenditures in education create a high return for both the employer and the employee, both the company and the individual should be *maximizing* the level of expenditure in education for employees, not artificially limiting those expenditures, as is being done today.

In reality, most companies manage expenditures for education as an expense, not as an investment, and employers seek to cap or control those expenditures under a benefits reporting line in the income statement. Meantime, while these internal controls are in place, companies are recruiting the required human assets in the open labor markets. The recruiting alternative is rapidly becoming far more difficult. Given the demographics related to the retirement of the baby boomers, recruiting inevitably will become yet more difficult and more expensive. Every company has seen the demographic data yet most are frozen, unable to deploy aggressive actions to deal with the inevitable demographics changes on the horizon. Why?

One answer resides in two cells of figure 23.1. While the return for education is objectively defined by millions of transactions in the labor markets the return from the thousands of training programs deployed by tens of thousands of firms is largely unmeasured. Given the absence of measurements and metrics related to human capital investment, the returns are largely guesses. As a result, investments in training (more than eighty billion dollars in 2006) were made blind—without precise information on the true business return. In the face of this uncertainty, companies do what is always done when faced with high uncertainty, they demand even higher expected returns to compensate for the uncertainty of the investment.

The second cell in figure 23.1 of importance to this alignment issue is in the intersection of education and risk. The risk dimension of the employer's investment in education investment is exactly the opposite for the employees under the most common approaches to tuition reimbursement. This misalignment of risk is the primary force behind capping or limiting investment in education even though the return for both the employee and the employer is *high and growing*. Significant increases in value creation for both the employee and the employer could result from alignment of the risk dimension to low for both the employer and the employee. Most organizations

135

attempt to manage the risk by restricting the expenditures. Some of the policies and practices that misalign risk exposure and incentives for the company are shown in table 23.1.

TABLE 23.1
Policies and Practices Traditionally Used to Manage Employer Education Risk

- ▶ Limit the employee "benefit" by capping the expenditures
  - ▶ $5,250 annual cap dictated by IRS ruling on taxable benefits
  - ▶ No or minimal annual "benefit" per employee
  - ▶ Artificial cap on reimbursement per credit hour
- ▶ Prescreen and select universities qualified to participate based upon alliance agreements
- ▶ Limit or restrict communication to employees about future needs
- ▶ Limit the total organization expenditure to a fixed annual budget
- ▶ Restrict salary action related to awarding of degree

In one form or another, every one of the policies and practices listed in table 23.1 is designed to limit the organization's risk. This is done to limit the level of the expenditures on the income statement (human capital investment as an expense) and to protect the exposure of the investing organization to the potential uncontrollable departure of employee from the organization—an event that takes both the invested capital and the potential return with the departing employee.

Corporations are desperately looking for good investment alternatives while simultaneously trying to recruit qualified people, but they continue to shovel cash out the door in the form of common stock buybacks. As the cash flows out of the company, investments in human capital are being strangled as expense control to create more income and cash. Human capital is an attractive investment alternative for cash usage, yet companies are restricting the level of such investments. These restrictions are not in response to demand for the human capital, but in response to the risk to the company related to such investments.

It is valuable to align the risk-return parameters for the company so that the employer and the employee have similar risk-return parameters. How can this be done?

The action to be taken is to convert the employer education investment risk from high to low. The other opportunity is to create retention incentives by linking increases in employee return to employee tenure with the company in the future. Both can be accomplished.

To secure the business benefits, the company needs to transfer the entire future risk of the investment capital to the employee. Since the company cannot control employee intent and the employees initially receive all of the benefit of the investment for their lifetime, the risk element of the investment decision needs to shift from the employer to the employees. This policy and practice shift does not appreciably alter the employee risk from low, but it does reduce the *immediate* return to the employee, but only under the event of early employee resignation. To maximize the capital available for human capital investment, the company needs to have some assurance of earning a return on that investment. This can only be done by equalizing the risk for both employee and employer.

From *ROI on Human Capital Investment*, table 4.2, page 26, the implications of the impact of the new policy and practice on the employee is captured. Table 23.2 below shows the analysis.

TABLE 23.2	
Improved Return to Employee	
Policy	Employee Return
Corporation pays zero tuition up front	400+ percent
Corporation pays 80 percent tuition	2,500+ percent

What table 23.2 shows is that the current widely used tuition assistance policies and practices of paying education investment costs up front simply improve the employee return from tremendous to extraordinarily fabulous. This increase in return to the employee represents a misallocation of investment resources relative to a more optimal mix. A far better risk-return mix is secured by the employer without significant degradation to the employee risk or eventual return. The details are shown in figure 23.2 for policies and practices that delay the dispensing of the human capital investment expenditure.

FIGURE 23.2

RETURN

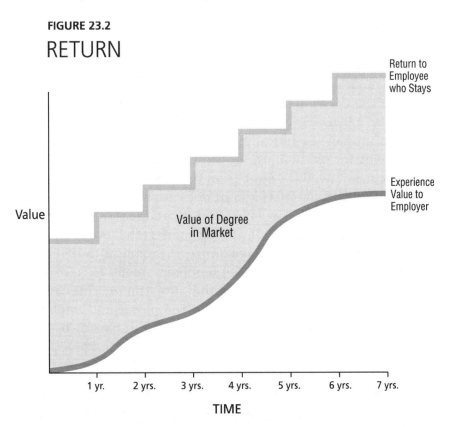

The value creation enhancement results from the elimination of employer risk. The line shows that the suggested policies "flat line" the employer risk at essentially zero over the entire time the employee is employed. The step line shows the increase in return for the employee as long as the employee receives repayment for their personally initiated human capital investment. The policies that create this result along with the associated restatement of risk-return are shown in table 23.3.

TABLE 23.3

Policies and Practices that Align Return-Risk

► Repay against employee education investment at a rate of $X per year as long as employee remains with company beginning one year after degree is awarded;

► Limit total repayment over the lifetime of the employee, not annually;

► Maximize communication to employees encouraging education;

► Remove restrictions on cost per course or universities attended;

► Design job/company/market related education in collaboration with universities.

FIGURE 23.3

IMPACT OF NEW POLICIES & PRACTICES

Employee / Employer

	RISK	RETURN
EDUCATION	Employee: Low	Employee: High and increasing over time
	Employer: Low	Employer: High and increasing over time*

*Each year the employee remains with company, the employer earns the value of the difference between compensation and the economic return to company, which is positive each year.

The change in human resource policies and practices recommended are often resisted on the belief that employees will be reluctant to invest their time and effort in education if the company contribution is not paid before the courses are taken. This is often argued based on a combination of cash flow and motivational factors. Under the recommended policies and practices, the cash flow issue is addressed through debt financing to the employee, an option widely supported by federal government programs as well as by a large number of private lenders specialized in student loans. The option to capitalize education with debt instruments held by the employee is widely available, thus eliminating the cash flow barrier.

The related issue of the perception of reduced employee motivation to take on the financial debt required to capitalize their education is not supported by the available data. At Bellevue University, a random sample of enrollment data for the degree completion programs showed that 70 percent of the cost to secure the degree was financed by the learner, not by a company. This demonstrates a willingness of a large number of adult learners to finance at least the majority of their own education. But there is another dimension to this discussion.

The basic rationale given for tuition payment up front is to motivate the employee to use the tuition assistance "benefit." At the same time, many organizations limit how aggressively the senior leaders communicate their desire for their employees to get an education. This reluctance to communicate is motivated by the desire to control total expenditures. The recommended policy is designed to equalize employee and employer risk. This may dissuade some employees from investing in themselves based on the fact that they have the financial responsibility for their own educational investment. A strong communication program with the new policies will more than offset the negative effect of the shift in the risk profile.

Employers that shift to the recommended human capital investment policies and practices have a potential competitive tool for both recruiting and retention. The company can easily adjust the rate at which the employee educational debt is retired in response to market conditions. That flexibility can be applied to debt held by a new employee being recruited into the firm in addition to impacting retention of existing employees. Under current corporate-wide tuition reimbursement benefit structures, implementation of changes in money distribution is cumbersome and inflexible at best.

By shifting the focus from education to training and the corresponding return—risk parameters for both employee and employer moves the focus to the second line of figure 23.1.

With training, the risk issue is not a disparity between employee and employer. Since training is more narrowly focused on specific business skills and, in general, has a far shorter shelf life than general education, the risk is assigned as low to moderate for both employer and employee. Indeed one historically used employer strategy to reduce employer risk has been to make the training so narrow and so specific as to significantly reduce the value of the skills to competitors.

With training, resources committed to rigorously measure the return are generally not committed in the first place. Unlike the education case, where the value of the bachelor's degree is set by millions of independent transactions in labor markets, training is highly diverse in nature, largely eliminating the opportunity to use wages in labor markets as the value creation measurement device. This leaves a huge void in the measurement of return from training. Cost effective methods to measure value creation or return on specific training programs are just being developed. The Human Capital Lab at Bellevue University is coming on stream with a mission to research and develop measurement and evaluation tools for companies to use. Capital Analytics of Durham, North Carolina is an operating company with the statistical analysis know-how to measure and evaluate complex return improvement issues and has done so for a growing portfolio of companies challenged to improve the return on their training expenditures.

In the arena of training returns, much work yet needs to be done. Nonetheless, there is ample evidence that significant progress can be made in this arena with the commitment of resources to do the work.

The last dimension of human capital investment relates to the experience gained by the employees as they successfully do their job. Let's accept the US Department of Labor estimates that as much as 70 percent of what an employee learns is acquired through "on-the-job training" as a reasonable approximation of value creation in the work place. The challenge then is to examine policies and practices related to managing return-risk related to experience.

As is the case for both training and education, the employee benefits directly and has little asset risk associated with the human capital created. The experience is theirs and it goes with them if they change jobs, however, as with training, the specific experience gained at one company has some depreciation component when applied at a new employer. The new employer is different in some ways from the old employer.

The one element of figure 23.1 that is important to examine is the experience risk to the employer. The prior chapter examined the asset value characteristics of experience gained over time. Briefly, what is shown is that experience is cumulative over time. What this means is that, on average, a highly experienced employee is considerably more valuable than a new hire.

The critical policy and practice implications of the experience factor is that it is very important for companies to actively work to retain their most experienced human assets. Losing an educated, trained, and experienced leader results in significantly greater future return loss than the loss from the departure of a new employee with only a few year's experience. While the observation is obvious, the challenge is to implement a strategy to deal with it.

There is one final factor worth considering in the experience dimension of human capital investment. Some employers control human capital investment expenditures related to training and education under the argument that their human capital development strategy is totally "on the job training."

24

The Financial Asymmetry of Recruiting vs. Retention

In the war for talent, recruitment vs. retention has several important competitive implications that impact human capital risk-return. Three dimensions where significant asymmetry exists are:

Company brand
Experience
Switching costs

From a competitive perspective, the company brand works against the most well-known brands—exactly the opposite of the case than that for poaching employees from a competitor. High brand reputation helps attract new recruits to the company as a result of the brand recognition. Individuals join companies, but leave their bosses. In the past, when recruitment was the primary human capital strategy, premium company brand worked to the advantage of the recruiting company. Individuals were attracted to the brand. In the future, competitors will be motivated to poach from high brand visible competitors precisely because they are highly visible.

There is strong evidence that the global supply of qualified individuals is inadequate to serve the existing demand for such individuals. A March, 2007 global survey of thirty-seven thousand employers in twenty-seven countries conducted by Manpower concluded that 41 percent of those surveyed were having trouble hiring the people they needed (*Business Week* April 9, 2007 p. 28). This strain between supply and demand reverses the brand advantage that existed when there was an adequate supply of skilled people, and recruiting meant simply finding the best candidate among the many available. The 41 percent result means that recruiters are having trouble finding qualified candidates, not merely searching to find the best from among many qualified. This changes the strategy for recruiting. The best place to find a qualified candidate is from within the brand organizations known for developing highly qualified people. With this reversal in market conditions, the high brand visibility that provided an advantage in recruiting new people forms a gigantic bull's eye for competitors looking to poach qualified employees.

Experience has a financial asymmetry between the current employer and the recruiter. Experience within a company includes such company specific characteristics as language, informal decision networks, culture, business models, history, etc. To the current employer, this company-specific experience has greater value than to the recruiting organization. As a result, investments to retain a current employee produce a higher return than recruiting expenditures used to attract an employee with similar tenure at a competitor.

The last area of financial asymmetry is in the area of switching costs. Switching costs are those noneconomic costs incurred by an employee to relocate themselves and their family to a new company in a new geographic area. See appendix C for a more detailed description of switching costs. The recruiting- retention asymmetry of these costs can be quite significant.

To fully understand the asymmetry of these switching costs, we need only examine a simple financial model shown in figure 24.1. For this analysis, assume that the prevailing labor market salary for position Alpha with ten years experience is fifty thousand dollars per year.

The gap between the current salary paid and the accepted salary offer represents the size of the switching cost to the employee. For the current employer, this gap represents an improvement in the return on any education and training investment, for the company does not have to pay the employee in the full market price to retain him/her. The switching cost differential works to the advantage of the current employer as a financial

FIGURE 24.1

RECRUITING vs. RETENTION

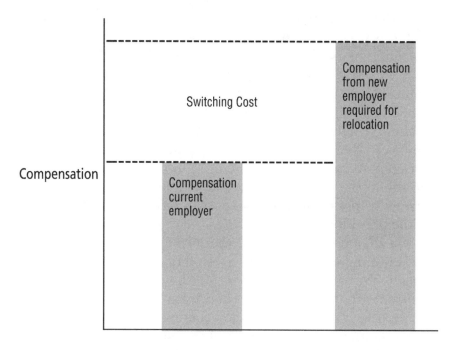

Compensation

Switching Cost

Compensation from new employer required for relocation

Compensation current employer

Note: With recruiting, the hiring company pays the switching cost.
With retention, the current employer avoids the switching cost.

reality that improves return on human capital investment when spent on current employees. The investing company does not have to pay full market value to retain the employee, in essence capturing the full switching cost as an increase in return from the investment made. The company has the potential to capture the full switching cost in operations.

The competitor seeking to recruit the newly trained/educated employee from their rival must actually pay a premium *above* the prevailing market price to compensate for the switching cost facing the employee being recruited. The reason we know this is because, in normal market conditions at the prevailing price X, the employee being recruited would already have moved from their current position at their current employer to the recruiting employer at market price X. The fact that the employee is still at the current employer is evidence that a significant switching cost is at play in the transaction. To recruit the employee away, the recruiting employer has to offer a premium above the prevailing market price to successfully recruit. In the limit, this premium probably has to be about as much above the prevailing salary X as the current salary is below the prevailing salary, i.e., in the limit the premium above X is approximately the magnitude of the switching cost itself.

Thus the switching cost creates a significant financial asymmetry between the current employer and the recruiting employer. The existence of the switching cost allows the current employer to pay below the prevailing market salary X and still retain the employee since the employee does not want to personally incur the switching cost to move to a new employer for the prevailing market price.

On the opposite side, the recruiting employer must offset the switching cost above the prevailing market price to compensate the targeted employee for the switching costs to be incurred with the move. What this means in terms of return and competitive strategy is that the economic benefit of switching costs operates to the advantage of the current employer and to the disadvantage of the recruiting employer. The bottom line of all of these financial asymmetries is that the value of retention exceeds the value of recruitment, all other things equal. This value proposition differential can do nothing but increase as the seventy million baby boomers draw down the supply of qualified people as they retire.

The irony in most companies is that the lion's share of focus, budget, and resources are in the area of recruitment not retention. A simple test is to identify and add up all of the individuals in the company who are directly or indirectly involved in recruiting activities. At the same time, add up all of the individuals in the company who have a primary responsibility for retention. It is almost certain that the recruitment head count significantly exceeds the head count for retention, if any are assigned to retention at all. The same analysis comparing recruitment expenditures (budgets) with retention expenditures (budgets) is an equally revealing and compelling exercise. As recruiting becomes more difficult in the next fifteen years, increases in recruiting expenditures will have to grow. At the same time, it is highly unlikely that expenditures directed toward retention will grow in proportion without a change in procedures and practices.

The bottom line is that retention has significant financial advantage over recruitment—an asymmetry that is structural. At the same time, the allocation of resources for recruitment vs. retention is highly likely to be exactly the opposite in most companies. Gathering the data and making the analysis is a rather low cost exercise. The potential competitive advantages to be had are significant, but it will take a shift in policies and practices to gain the potential value creation benefits.

25 Increasing the Value Created

Talent, skills, knowledge, and experience are the key components of human capital. All contribute to value creation in an increasingly uncertain world. The policies, practices, and procedures that organizations follow to impact these critical components directly impact the magnitude of the value created.

The form of the knowledge is important. What is clear is that time is required to gain experience, the 70 percent component of knowledge identified by the US Department of Labor. In addition, the investment in the development of skills and knowledge takes time. Learning is not instantaneous. Skills, knowledge, and experience are all gained over time. It is an investment—a commitment of current resources to produce a future value. Targeted human capital investment to create knowledge has the potential to further improve the impact on business outcomes. An example follows.

In the case of developing leaders for a large retailer, one human capital investment alternative is to commit some of the enterprise cash to an education that leads to a degree in astrophysics. While such a degree might be high in prestige, it provides little knowledge useful about how to lead an organization composed of retail employees. The most valuable human capital investment option is the development of skills, knowledge, and experience most directly relevant to the actual value creation context being faced during the future time period(s). While the

149

value creation options appear so completely obvious, few human resource departments actually do it.

The "contextualizing" of training and education is a highly efficient investment action to increase the value potential resulting from the human capital investment. By matching the learning with the future operating issues to be faced by the employee, the value impact of the original human capital investment is increased.

There is another option to increase the future value creation potential of current human capital investments. In the face of the restricted supply of talented, educated, and experienced professionals already documented, the enhancement of the value created from human capital investments today depends heavily on the retention of those human capital assets as more and more competitors seek to lure away a company's "most important asset." Retention is critical.

Employees, employers, and stockholders all have the potential to create far greater value from significantly increased levels of investment in human capital than the $109 billion spent in 2006. America has the potential to gain competitive advantage in the global economy and individual companies have the potential to gain important competitive advantage in their markets. These are bold assertions. Risk management is at the heart of the issue.

In the end, the business goal is to give C-suite executives a better road map to make human capital investment decisions. Equally important is the goal of providing stockholders with the rationale and supporting evidence required to give those executives time to change policies, procedures, and practices in ways that take advantage of the insights related to intangible assets and value creation in the twenty-first-century global "knowledge" economy. The C-suite executives will need this time to fend off the assault of the short term pressures as they attempt to redirect the focus beyond next quarter's reported earnings per share.

Appendix A

Private Nonresidential Fixed Investments

Source: US Department of Commerce: Bureau of Economic Analysis

STRUCTURES

Commercial and health care

Manufacturing

Power and Communication

Mining exploration, shafts and wells

Other structures

EQUIPMENT AND SOFTWARE

Information processing equipment and software

Computers and peripheral equipment

Software

Other

INDUSTRIAL EQUIPMENT

Transportation equipment

Other equipment

Appendix B

Market Stock Price to Book Value

Source: TD Ameritrade online 2/5/07

	Price to book value
Halliburton	4.06
Baker Hughes	4.39
Schlumberger	7.38
Intel	3.33
Cisco Systems	6.45
The Home Depot	3.01
Lowes	3.44
Google	8.67
Apple	6.49
General Electric	3.33
Wachovia	1.54
Microsoft	8.06
Procter and Gamble	3.23
Verizon	2.32
Altria	4.57

Caterpillar	6.19
Medtronic	6.02
IBM	5.33
Disney	2.28
Boeing	14.99
Dow Chemical	2.32
Union Pacific	1.81
Conagra Foods	2.75
Accenture	18.24
Prudential Financial	1.87
Lockheed Martin	6.09
United Technologies	3.95
Wal-Mart	3.41
Average	5.20

5.20 is the price to book value comparable to graph in figure 1.4

Appendix C

Switching Costs

Even as new software has more functions and has a lower purchase price, it is extremely difficult for a company to replace old software with new. Employees are familiar with the old. The costs to change company processes and retrain the work force are called switching costs—i.e., the hidden costs to switch. Employees considering a new position with a new firm face similar switching costs. The nature of the switching costs for the employee can be best understood through a hypothetical example involving Jack Armstrong.

Jack is a thirty-eight-year-old married man. He and his wife have two teenage children. He currently works for company X in city Y. The new job offer is at a salary 30 percent higher than his current salary at company X and there is a $30,000 one-time signing bonus. The problem is that the offering company Z is in a different state approximately nine hundred and fifty miles from his current residence. Jack is anguishing over the decision.

The anguish is over all of the switching costs related to taking the new job. The list begins with his home ownership. His current residence has a mortgage rate of 4.5 percent per year, and the current market mortgage rate is approaching 6 percent per annum. In addition to the increased mortgage rate, the family must face the sale of their existing residence, find a new home in the new location, negotiate contracts, and probably purchase new furnishings to fit into the house.

At work, Jack will have to sever the personal relationships in his network of colleagues built over the years. Research shows that the informal organization is even more important than the formal organization chart. Jack will have to build a new informal network at firm Z. Over the years, Jack has gained

extensive experience about the language, culture, and processes of his current employer.

While all of these switching costs are real, they represent
only a fraction of the total. The lion's share of what Jack faces
involves his family and their relationships. Jill, his wife has a well
paying job and has recently been promoted to a new executive
position. In her new position, she actually makes more than Jack
does. For Jack to switch, he has to ask his wife to give up her
informal network and all the accumulated experience with her
current employer. She faces losing everything Jack is facing,
doubling that part of the switching costs for the family.

The conversation between Jack and Jill is an adult conversation, one they can have somewhat objectively between each
other. The teenage kids are another matter altogether. Even if
Jack and Jill can reconcile their own feelings about their own
personal switching costs, any decision to move the family will
ultimately involve the emotions of the teenage girls. For the
teenagers, the contemplated move means giving up all of their
relationships with their friends. They are faced with leaving their
friends exactly at the time in their lives when friends are most
important to them. It is the switching cost Jack and Jill will only
have even after the two adults have reconciled their own feelings
about their personal switching costs.

In the end, human capital switching costs are highly asym-
metric and work to the benefit of the current employer. For the
new company in the new state, the cash offer must compensate
Jack and his entire family to overcome the switching costs of the
contemplated move. Jack's current employer does not have to
incur any of this out-of-pocket expense to retain Jack.

In the end, switching costs represent a significant economic
advantage for the current employer. The key policy, procedure,
and practice actions are to recognize that the switching costs
actually exist and use some of the real cash advantage to reinvest
in the employee to increase skills and knowledge while simultaneously reducing turnover.

Appendix D

Education Investment Impact on Retention

Three well-documented studies show the positive impact of tuition reimbursement on retention. All three studies lead to a conclusion opposite that of prior research that was conducted in the 1960s. That earlier work by Becker stated that training specific to the firm reduces turnover because the skills are specific to the firm. The theory of that work also states that the favorable impact on turnover does not hold for general education (accredited degrees) because these skills are transferable to other employers. According to Becker's theory, offering employees general skills training would increase turnover.

Here is a summary of the three studies done in real organizations that show tuition reimbursement actually decreases turnover.

Study 1: "The Effect of Tuition Reimbursement on Turnover: A Case Study" by Colleen N. Flaherty.

This research was done at Stanford University and published as a working paper by the National Bureau of Economic Research (NBER). The research was done at a nonprofit organization over two years, involving both supervisory and nonsupervisory personnel. Using sophisticated statistical analysis techniques, Flaherty concluded that participation by those employees hired after the tuition assistance program implemented reduced their probability of leaving within five years by more than 50 percentage points.

Study 2: "You Paid for the Skills, Now Keep Them: Tuition Reimbursement and Voluntary Turnover" by George S. Benson, David Finegold, and Susan Albers Mohrman and published in the Academy of Management Journal.

This is a huge study involving more than nine thousand highly skilled employees at one company. The data used is longitudinal data spanning the period 1996 through 2000. What the research showed was that, when combined with actions related to salary and promotion, education significantly reduced turnover among those employees using the tuition reimbursement benefit to earn a bachelor degree. Employees who took any type of class through tuition reimbursement were 60 percent less likely than a nonparticipant to quit the company.

Study 3

Verizon Wireless, under the tuition reimbursement program administered by Dorothy Martin, routinely measures and tracks the impact of tuition reimbursement on four business parameters including: recruiting, promotion, performance, and retention. The data and supporting analysis shows that among the approximately sixty-eight thousand Verizon Wireless employees, the turnover among the approximately twelve thousand employees taking advantage of the company's tuition reimbursement "benefit" is reduced by more than 50 percent relative to the general employment population.

Summary of All Three Studies:

All three studies independently draw the same conclusion. The relationship between tuition reimbursement and turnover is measurable and significant. In all three studies, the turnover among those enrolled in accredited degree seeking courses was reduced by the same order of magnitude; about 50 percent. A 50 percent reduction in turnover has significant human capital implications for companies.

Appendix E

Cash and Value

In value creation, cash is a means, not an end. No one eats cash, drinks cash, wears cash, or sleeps on cash. Cash cannot warm a home, transport a child, educate a human, or heal a wound. Cash can only create value when transformed from a pile of paper to something of value to humans. Thus, even though financial markets define success using cash as the measurement, the cash by itself has no enduring end value no matter how fervently advocates praise its "value."

To see the position of cash in the value chain, a brief exercise is revealing. Confronted with the need to plan for thirty days of survival, you are given the opportunity to stock up physical assets (your balance sheet) for a month in severe winter weather. At the end of the thirty days, any leftover assets of the items are returned to the stocking point. The list of assets from which to pick includes:

Food
Water
Warm clothing
Shelter
Fuel for heat
Bedding
Cash

The decision allowed is the selection of six of the seven items. The six items selected are those to be taken into the thirty-day winter period. In this first example, there is no second step in the decision process. The selection is once and done.

A rational person will select the first six items on the list, leaving cash behind. That is the highest value choice precisely

159

because cash has no end value in the context of the expected future. The first six items on the list have value to survival and comfort. Cash provides neither.

To further calibrate the relative value of the items, merely consider the choice of all the cash in the US Treasury, but no water. In this exercise, water clearly has far more value than even unlimited quantities of cash precisely because water is far more valuable to life than is cash.

Now let's change the example in two basic ways. The first change is to allow the decision to include a market. A market is a means to exchange any item on the list for another item on the list. For simplicity, we look at a single transforming action. The same reasoning extends to an infinite number of such transactions. In this modification, the market is a means to transform one item into another in an action of buying or selling—i.e., a market transaction.

So, under this market modification, what is now allowed is the selection of six items from the list and then one market transaction before the thirty-day winter survival period begins. Table E.1 shows buy-sell combinations in terms of value created from each. For simplicity, a sale involves the sale of all of the item in the asset class. Fractional transactions are not possible as a matter of simplicity even though a fractional transaction derives the same result.

TABLE E.1

VALUE CREATION		
Give Up	**Get**	**Value Change**
Water	Cash	Decrease
Food	Cash	Decrease
.	Cash	.
.	Cash	.
.	Cash	.
Shelter	Cash	Decrease
Cash	More food	Increase

The point of the actions and results shown in table E.1 is that every transaction that moves from any of the first six items to cash leaves the decision maker with less value. *All* transactions resulting with more cash leaves the decision maker with *less* value than before the market transaction was completed.

Even with this form of market, the asset of cash has no value in the end. Cash only has value potential when there is a transaction that allows the exchange between the current composition of assets before the final state. Thus cash has value when there is the potential for a market transaction, in the final state, cash has no value. Under those conditions, cash has value as a result of its universal nature and ease of transaction relative to transactions involving all of the other asset categories. The value of cash results from its ease of exchange relative to the transaction between asset classes.

There are circumstances that increase the value of cash, all of which relate to the transactions of the market. Before the beginning of the thirty-day survival period, the value of cash increases in direct proportion to the number of transactions that are allowed to take place before the beginning of the thirty-day period. Because cash is totally indifferent to the composition of the other assets, having cash when an unlimited number of transactions are possible allows adjustment of the asset composition as often as desired prior to the beginning of the thirty-day survival period.

For example, the decision maker has the option to adjust the amount of food and water in the asset composition, something they would want to do were they to find out that a loved one was suddenly to join them during the thirty-day period. Thus the relative value of cash increases with the increase in the number of unforeseen events that might occur between the first selection and the beginning of the thirty-day winter period. So the first instance of cash value increase is the increase in the potential number of situational variables that might change between the first transaction and the last transaction. In this case, increased cash has increasing value as a risk mitigating asset in the face of uncertain future states.

Another factor that increases the relative value of cash is the expansion of the market to include transactions between other asset holders in the market. An increase in the number of asset holders gives cash the expanded value of being able to acquire even more of any given asset beyond that in the original choice set. The more participants in the market, the greater is the relative value of cash.

Another factor that increases the relative value of cash is the lowering of the transaction cost to exchange cash for another asset class. This further enhances the value of cash relative to barter by lowering the relative cost of a cash transaction relative to a barter transaction.

Yet another fact that increases the relative value of cash is the changing of the rules to allow transactions during the thirty-day period. In this case, cash at the beginning of the thirty-day period gives the greatest flexibility to alter the asset composition during the thirty-day period based upon emerging circumstances unknowable at the beginning of the thirty-day period.

Finally, if the asset stocks can be known through a list on a computer screen, the transaction can be completed on that same computer screen without ever having to go to the asset location. Thus the expansion of the linked global computer network increases the relative value of cash in a global market where the number of asset holders is increasing. When these factors are summarized, relative value of cash is increased when an infinite number of transactions are allowed. It is easy to see why cash has gained relative value in the global market. Table E.2 summarizes the attributes of such transactions that increase the relative value of cash.

TABLE E.2

CHANGING FACTORS CHANGING RELATIVE VALUE		
Example	from	to
Reduced transaction cost		
Broker Fees	$ per hundred shares	$9.95 unlimited
Increased number asset holders		
Wealth creation	Domestic markets	Global markets
Increased number of changes		
Rapid technology change	10 year product cycles	10 month product cycles
New competitors	Domestic markets	Global markets
Ubiquitous information	Paper reports	Linked computer system
Increased asset value uncertainty		
Hydrocarbon reserves	Primitive geology/seismology	Advanced computer modeling
Human capital	Stable linked to balance sheet	Independent free agents

What table E.2 shows are some of the factors of an expanding global economy serviced by a worldwide computer network. The information age increases options while reducing transaction costs. In the world we now live in, the relative value of cash is increasing as a hedge against the increasing complexity of markets and the associated uncertainty created by that complexity. Under all of these circumstances, the relative value of cash exists *only* in the context of a transaction, i.e., where a market exists.

In all cases, the relative value of cash is as a means. No amount of increase in the complexity of the markets (transactions) changes the fact that cash has zero value as an end. Were global financial markets to break down due to a loss of confidence, the relative value of cash in a world where transactions could not take place would decline. Under such a scenario, a case of potatoes would suddenly have much greater value than a roll of one hundred dollar bills.

It is the existence of fluid markets with growing trans-actional opportunities that increases the relative value of cash. In the face of stable efficient markets, the relative value of cash is preserved. When examined in the face of end values, the advantages of cash disappear entirely.

It is now worthwhile to return to the issue of creating value, especially with regard to human capital. In this case, the examination is of end value. Return to the original conditions of the decision before the beginning of the thirty-day winter period when no changes during the thirty-day period are allowed. For simplicity, we return to the original asset list and one transaction.

Food
Water
Warm Clothing
Shelter
Fuel for heat
Bedding
Cash

We also return to the original transaction options defined by table E.2 with the addition of one transaction option—the exchange of cash for more fuel for heat shown with the arrow in table E.3 below

TABLE E.3

VALUE CREATION		
Give up	Get	Value change
Water	Cash	Decrease
Food	Cash	Decrease
.		.
.		.
.		.
Shelter	Cash	Decrease
Cash	More food	Increase
Cash	More fuel for heat	Increase

164

The exchange of cash for more fuel creates new value. This is value not even available on the original asset list. By using the cash to increase the reserves of fuel, the decision invents insurance against the risk that the winter weather during the thirty-day period turns out to be colder than forecast. Through this innovative use of cash, new value is created through an option that did not even exist on the original list of assets. By knowing that the severity of the winter weather might be highly variable, purchasing insurance against the variability created value even in the absence of more complete information about the unknowable temperature during the upcoming thirty-day period. Through innovation and critical thinking, the decision created value with no change in the original assets listed.

This innovative action is particularly important relative to investment in human capital. The human capital asset of value was the knowledge of the variability of the weather and the associated threat of the consequences of running out of fuel before the end of the thirty-day period. The innovative decision required knowledge about the decision circumstances as well as the history of the environment being faced.

The key human capital elements creating this innovation are the synthesis and analysis of data about the weather and critical thinking skills to create an alternative that did not previously exist.

First, the knowledge had to be acquired *before* the time of the actual single transaction. Since the knowledge had to be present at the time of the final transaction, the acquisition of that knowledge could not take place simultaneously with the transaction itself. The acquisition of the specific knowledge represents an investment in human capital made before the transaction point. How long before the transaction the human capital investment had to be made depended upon the complexity of the knowledge required to make the best insurance decision. The more complex the situation, the greater the lead time needed to acquire the knowledge needed. Thus, the human capital investment required to make the decision was necessary to even make possible the risk mitigating transaction represented by the exchange of cash. This is a specific case where human capital investment creates value in the end situation.

There is a new set of circumstances where a prior investment in human capital in the form of know-how creates value. In this example, no transactions are allowed prior to the beginning of the thirty-day period, but an unlimited number of transactions are allowed during the thirty-day period and assets can be retained after the end of the thirty-day period.

In this situation, the external environment is changing rapidly with significant changes in transaction prices *during* the thirty-day period. Here, knowledge of market opportunities to buy sell and exchange assets creates the potential to increase the value of the physical assets by changing the mix of assets based upon their evolving relative prices in the markets. Knowledge about where to find market information about availability, prices, and costs enhances the market value of the assets held. Just as in the case of cash, the relative value of human capital is increased by the same global market that increased the relative value of cash, namely increasing complexity, which increases the uncertainty of future markets. In the case of cash, holding that asset serves as a market hedge against the risk related to the increasing uncertainty. In the case of human capital, we have the asset of knowledge, which serves as a foundation for making innovative decisions as the unknowable situations actually emerge. The decision-making capability represented by the talent, skills, knowledge, and experience (the human capital) of the decision maker increases the likelihood that the actual decisions increase value in the end. The fact that the human capital is not listed on the balance sheet is irrelevant to the value created by the actual transactions made, either before or during the thirty-day period.

Thus while cash has increasing relative value in a world of widely available information, growing uncertainty, and expanding markets, the capabilities of human capital become increasingly important to value creation outcomes. The global economy dynamics increase the importance of human capital in value creation.

Index

turnover, 33, 39, 49-50, 52-55,
60, 63, 75, 88, 115,
127-128, 131-132, 156-158
Tversky, Amos, 46

US Census Bureau, 38
US Department of Labor, 92, 98,
129, 141, 149

venture capitalists, 77
Verizon Wireless, 153, 158

Wall Street Journal, 78
Welsh, Jack, 63

Yahoo, 53